# RETIREMENT PLANNING FOR EVERY LIFE STAGE

Junius Ellis
and the Editors of MONEY

## Other MONEY Books by Junius Ellis

♦ *Money Adviser 1996*
♦ *Investing for a Secure Retirement*
♦ *Making Money With Mutual Funds*

# Contents

To order MONEY Magazine, call Customer Service at 800-633-9970
or write to MONEY, P.O. Box 60001, Tampa, Florida 33660-0001.

*Retirement Planning For Every Life Stage*

**Editor:** Junius Ellis
**Designer:** Laura Ierardi, LCI Design
**Cover:** Illustration by Nigel Holmes

# 1

# Heed Your Financial Life Cycle

Whatever you've heard about retirement, rest assured that it's never too late to start planning for yours. The process ideally begins after you go to work in your middle to late twenties. That's when you will lay the foundation for your retirement by saving for financial goals nearer at hand, such as buying your first home and raising a family. By getting into the habit of saving at least 5% of your salary, you will do more to prepare for the future than you would by worrying about pensions, Social Security and the like. The time to begin building a nest egg is when you are in your thirties and forties. The primary aim then is to put aside upwards of 10% of your income, including maximum contributions to such tax-deferred accounts as 401(k) savings plans.

The main objective behind saving so diligently for retirement is financial independence. The price is the increasingly complex planning that's required to amass, protect and pass on wealth to the next generation. Keep in mind that retirement planning is no longer a concern primarily of people who are within five to 10 years of calling it quits. Every stage of life, from your thirties to your forties and fifties, demands different strategies and a keen appreciation of today's major trends.

Consider that children recently born in America will turn 65 in a society where one in five persons is that age or older. This will be the inexorable result of demographic changes that are unfolding all around us. The age seesaw of our population, which was once weighted by the young, will tilt heavily toward the old. The main reasons? Baby boomers are rapidly maturing, and the average life span is increasing. Projected life expectancy at birth could reach 80 by the year 2000, compared with 70 in 1965. This trend means that the typical married couple already has more living parents than children. It means that spouses will spend more years together after their children have left home than they did raising them. It means the average woman will spend more years caring for her aging mother than she will have spent caring for a child.

What's more, it means a new set of hazards can trip you up on the path to a secure retirement. This chapter and others that follow will help put you on the right course. We'll help you determine how much your retirement lifestyle will cost and what you will need to save to create your nest egg. We'll also show you the smartest way to invest your savings; assess a corporate severance or early retirement package; and blunt the Internal Revenue Service's potentially big bite. But first you need to learn the new rules of the game.

**Expect to live 30 years in retirement.** That's nearly the life expectancy of today's 50-year-olds and may be more years than they spent working. A half-century ago they would have been lucky to reach 73. At the same time, the average retirement age has declined. Roughly 52% of workers now file for Social Security at age 62, up from 35% in 1978. But there is an increasing chance that a corporate buyout could force you to rewrite your retirement plan. Some 29% of firms surveyed by the American Management Association used voluntary separation packages to slash their payrolls during a recent 12-month period, up from 17% five years ago. The companies that used these programs included giants like IBM that were once regarded as lifetime employers.

**Don't rely on the firm or Feds.** Financial planners often tell clients to think of retirement finances as a three-legged stool. One leg is Social Security. The second is your pension. And the third is personal savings. Retirees once could count on all three legs to remain steady. Today, however, Social Security and employer-financed pensions are getting shaky for many people. That means the third leg, personal savings, has to bear more weight.

Social Security will replace about 42% of wages if your earnings during your career averaged $21,800 a year but only about 27% if your average salary was $60,600. And this most sacred of middle-class entitlements is being chipped away. In recent years, the portion of your Social Security payments subject to federal income tax has climbed from 50% to 85% if your total income (including half of your Social Security payout) tops $44,000 for married couples and $34,000 for singles. The age at which you can expect to receive full Social Security benefits is also slated to rise, from 65 today to 66 in 2005 and 67 in 2022. With future outlays by the Social Security trust fund projected to outpace revenues by 2025, many retirement experts can foresee further cutbacks in the next decade or so. Among the likely options are another boost in the age for receiving benefits, a reduction in beneficiaries' annual cost-of-living increases—or perhaps both.

If you're lucky, you'll be among the 40% of the work force whose Social Security checks will be supplemented by traditional defined-benefit pensions. These plans provide a fixed monthly payout, typically 30% of your final salary if you work 30 years or more. Even if your company offers a defined-benefit pension, you may have reason to worry about its safety. Underfunding at federally insured pension plans recently totaled $53 billion, up from $38 billion a year earlier, according to the federal Pension Benefit Guarantee Corporation. While these pensions are federally protected if your company folds or can't afford to stay in business without terminating its plan, you may not recoup all your promised pension benefits. And the reason is that federal insurance recently was capped at less than $31,000 a year.

Some companies have replaced traditional pensions with defined-contribution plans such as 401(k)s, which rely heavily on worker savings. Moreover, about half of workers with traditional pensions are covered by supplementary defined-contribution plans, up from roughly 33% in 1980. This reflects a basic shift from the view that the employer will take care of you to one where the employer will give you some retirement plans so you can take care of yourself. A 401(k) works well if you tend to job hop because you can take your retirement savings with you (provided that you've worked three to five years for your old employer). Traditional pensions aren't as portable and can penalize job hoppers because benefits depend on years of service. For a complete menu of your choices, check out our table "The Rundown on Retirement Plans" on page 10.

A 401(k), however, is less secure than a pension, which pays you a fixed amount each month, no matter how the markets perform. A 401(k)'s rate of return and your account's ultimate value are not guaranteed and partly depend on how astutely you invest. Also, 401(k)s tend to be invested too conservatively and earn lower investment returns than traditional pensions do. And many people spend their 401(k) savings when they change jobs, instead of hanging on to the money until retirement. Worse, companies tend to put less money in 401(k)s than in pensions. Employer contributions to defined-benefit plans run 10% to 12% of pay. Yet even in generous 401(k)s, employee contributions and employer matches might total 7% of pay. The chief reason is that younger and lower-paid workers can't afford to put much money in 401(k)s. The lower the amount, the less companies contribute.

## Take charge of your future. Statistics suggest most
workers aren't saving enough. America's 77 million baby boomers between the ages of 30 and 48 are now socking away just a third of what they need to maintain their standard of living in retirement, notes Stanford University economist Douglas Bernheim. People often put off saving for retirement so they can more easily achieve other goals, such as educating their children. The longer you wait, however, the more you jeopardize your future

# The Rundown on Retirement Plans

| PLAN | AVAILABLE TO | BEST FOR | MAXIMUM CONTRIBUTION | TAX BREAK ON CONTRIBUTIONS/ EARNINGS |
|------|-------------|----------|---------------------|-------------------------------------|
| 401(k) | Employees of for-profit businesses | Everyone who qualifies | 15% of salary, up to $9,500[1] in 1996 | Yes/Yes |
| 403(b) | Employees of nonprofit organizations | Everyone who qualifies | 20% of gross salary or $9,500, whichever is less | Yes/Yes |
| IRA | Anyone with earned income | Those who don't have company pension plans or who have put the maximum into their company plans | 100% of wages up to $2,000; $2,250 if joint with spouse | Sometimes/Yes |
| SEP | The self-employed and employees of small businesses | Self-employed person who is a sole proprietor | 13% of net self-employment income, or $22,500, whichever is less[2] | Yes/Yes |
| PROFIT-SHARING KEOGH | The self-employed and employees of unincorporated small businesses | Small-business owner who is funding a plan for himself and employees | Same as SEP[2] | Yes/Yes |
| MONEY-PURCHASE KEOGH | Same as profit-sharing Keogh | Small-business owner who wants to shelter more than allowed by profit-sharing Keogh | 20% of net self-employment income, or $30,000, which-ever is less[2] | Yes/Yes |
| DEFINED-BENEFIT KEOGH | Same as profit-sharing Keogh | Self-employed person nearing retirement who needs to set aside a high percentage of income | Maximum needed to fund $120,000[1] annual benefit, or three years' average income, whichever is less[2] | Yes/Yes |
| VARIABLE ANNUITY | Anyone | Someone who has put the maximum into other plans and won't need the money for 10 years | None | No/Yes |
| FIXED ANNUITY | Anyone | Someone who has put the maximum into other plans and shuns risk | None | No/Yes |

**Notes:** [1]Amount increases yearly with inflation rate. [2]Small-business owners fund the SEPs and Keoghs of their employees. [3]Percentage of employee's contribution [4]Some plans charge $20 to $30 annual administrative fees. [5]Surrender charges last six to eight years and typically decline by 1% a year. [6]All plans are subject to 10% income tax penalty, except in case of death or disability.

**Heed Your Financial Life Cycle**

| MATCHING CONTRIBUTIONS | CHARGES/FEES | EARLY WITHDRAWAL[6] | NUMBER OF INVESTMENT OPTIONS |
|---|---|---|---|
| Anywhere from 0% to 100%,[3] but typically only up to 6% of salary | Depends on plan/annual expenses of 1% to 1.5% of assets[4] | Only in case of hardship | Three to 10, typically, depending on your employer's plan |
| Generally not available | Depends on plan/annual expenses of 1% to 3% of assets | Only in case of hardship and employee contributions only | One to 10, typically, depending on your employer's plan |
| None | Depends on investment/ zero to $50 annual fee | Always permitted | Nearly everything except real estate, collectibles and other hard assets |
| None | Depends on investment/ $10 to $30 a year | Always permitted | Same as IRA |
| None | Depends on investment/ up to $2,000 in annual administrative expenses | Always permitted | Unlimited |
| None | Same as profit-sharing Keogh | Always permitted | Unlimited |
| None | Depends on investment/ $2,000 to $4,000 annual expenses | Always permitted | Unlimited |
| None | 6% to 8% surrender charges[5]/annual expenses of 2% to 2.2% of assets | Always permitted | Anywhere from one to 22, but typically nine |
| None | Surrender charges of 6% to 8%[5] | Always permitted | One |

well-being. Let's say that you're a 40-year-old with $20,000 in savings. If you put $2,000 a year in a 401(k) or other tax-deferred account, you would accumulate $220,000 by age 62, assuming that you earn roughly an 8% annual return. If you wait five years longer to start saving, you'll have just $176,000.

**Protect against inflation.** Prices are expected to increase at a modest rate of around 3% this year. Yet you can't afford to gamble that inflation won't be considerably higher when you retire. Even at today's levels, price increases eventually take a big bite out of your benefit check. Over 15 years, 3% annual inflation will shrink the value of a $2,000-a-month pension by more than a third, while 4% inflation will cut it nearly in half. Most company pensions don't rise with annual inflation. Roughly a quarter of large firms surveyed by consultants Greenwich Associates have never increased retirement payouts, while another 28% haven't boosted benefit checks in at least seven years. Thus, early in retirement, a pension and Social Security might meet 60% to 80% of your needs. But in 12 or 15 years, as inflation eats into the value of your pension, they may provide only 40% of the income you need.

**Keep expectations realistic.** Over the past decade or so, earning double-digit annual returns has been a snap. Stocks in the Standard & Poor's 500 index returned a yearly average of about 15%, and bonds maturing in five years gained about 11%, according to Ibbotson Associates, a Chicago investment research firm. Over the next five years, however, pension plan sponsors expect the S&P 500 to return only 9% annually and professionally managed bond funds just 7%. This means you'll have to save more to keep your retirement comfortable. In addition, you can't afford to play it too safe in investing your stash. About 27% of 401(k) assets lately were invested in low-risk, low-yielding GICs (guaranteed investment contracts), according to data compiled by Greenwich Associates. The better choice is stocks or stock funds, which provide bigger annual returns over time and help keep your portfolio ahead of inflation.

**Plan to keep on working.** It's a mistake to think of retirement as a sudden exit from the work force. As many as half of all retirees take less demanding jobs to smooth their move from careers to retirement. By working in retirement, you enable your savings to keep compounding, and you delay the time you'll need to tap them, perhaps until age 62 or 65. Even more retirees are expected to work in the future because company early-out offers are forcing many employees to retire before they have built adequate savings. Still, retiring in comfort is clearly attainable. All you have to do is pay attention to the new rules and weigh the advice provided in subsequent chapters of this book.

 ## Will Your Stash Last a Lifetime?

Few working Americans are taking the steps needed to turn their retirement aspirations into reality. That's the sobering conclusion of a MONEY poll conducted with Oppenheimer Management, a Wall Street investment firm. Our poll found 73% of adults between the ages of 21 and 64 expect to retire comfortably and 74% plan to do so before 65. Yet less than half of those questioned are investing in assets that are likely to provide the money they will need. To cite one disturbing fact, nearly as many have purchased lottery tickets for retirement (39%) as have invested in stocks (43%).

So just how much money will be required to ease you on down the road? Take a 35-year-old man earning $50,000 who lacks a company pension or savings plan. He will need to amass the equivalent of $1 million over the next 30 years to retire comfortably at age 65 and support his lifestyle to age 90. Yet 73% of respondents estimated their investment needs to be lower (usually 33% to 50% lower). Moreover, three out of five believe they will be able to live on less than 70% of their pre-retirement income—the minimum amount, according to many experts. As a result, the typical American could end up with less than half the money he or she will need in retirement. What to do?

**Get serious about planning.** The nation's largest single age cohort, those 77 million baby boomers mentioned earlier, will not glide gently into their golden years unless they step up their savings pace. For one thing, they probably will receive a less generous stipend from Social Security than their parents' generation. By 2030, when most baby boomers will have retired, there will be only two workers paying into Social Security for every retiree, vs. about 3.2 to 1 today. Unless Washington beefs up Social Security financing or reduces its benefits, the system will likely start running in the red by the year 2025. Dwindling Social Security payments are not the only hurdle confronting baby boomers. Rising taxes are likely if Uncle Sam does not cut spending, notes economist Laurence Kotlikoff at Boston University. Says he: "If Congress doesn't take action to cut the deficit and slow health care spending, the baby boom generation could face tax hikes of up to 40% in retirement." Increasing health care costs also seem certain for baby boomer retirees because, sooner or later, Congress must arrest the ballooning budgets for Medicare and Medicaid. Reduced corporate retirement benefits are likely too as businesses slash costs to remain competitive.

Affording a gracious retirement will be even more difficult for women because they tend to live longer than do men. Today's middle-aged female is likely to live to the age of 80, compared with 74 for her male counterpart. As a result, a woman needs a larger nest egg than a man to maintain the same level of investment income through retirement. At the same time, she may have a harder time accumulating what she needs. Women earn 30% less than men, on average, and they are also less likely to hold jobs that offer a company retirement plan. Single and divorced women are most at risk because they are less likely to share a spouse's benefits and full Social Security income. An Oppenheimer Management study found that the typical single woman who is in her thirties and lacks a pension will retire with only about 20% of the income she really needs.

**Scrutinize your budget.** Do you really need to eat out three nights a week? Or even twice? Can you forgo that luxury coupe for the less costly sedan? And what about basic, money-saving moves such as shopping at warehouse clubs or improving your home's energy efficiency? Many families can save 10% or more just by cutting back on unnecessary expenditures. Before you start locking away that newfound money, however, make sure that you have built up an emergency cash reserve equivalent to three to six months' worth of expenses. You should keep that money in a safe place, such as a CD (certificate of deposit) or money-market fund, where you can get your hands on it quickly without penalty. Once you get your savings plan under way, keep it in the groove by signing up for an automatic investing plan, authorizing your fund company to transfer a fixed amount every month from your bank account to funds of your choice. Most fund groups offer such automatic investing programs. And many of them will waive their investment minimum if you agree to make monthly contributions of as little as $50.

**Shelter your nest egg.** A tax-deferred savings plan can help speed you along the road to retirement wealth. You get an immediate tax deduction for your contribution. And, over the years, the effects of tax-deferred compounding can be awesome. Here's an example. If a 35-year-old earning $60,000 a year routinely contributes 6% of his salary to a taxable account earning 8% a year, he would have $185,744 by age 65 (assuming a 30% tax rate). If he were to invest that money in a tax-deferred account, he would amass a hefty $407,820. Even if he then withdrew the entire amount and paid taxes at a 30% rate on the proceeds, he would be ahead by 54%. Many investors, however, don't take full advantage of their opportunities to shelter money. One survey of employers by accountant KPMG Peat Marwick found that only about 60% of eligible workers participate in 401(k)s even though 85% of employers match their contributions (typically 50¢ on the dollar up to a specified percentage of salary). Thus if your employer offers a 401(k), put in the maximum allowed. If you can't afford that much, at least put in enough to get the full matching amount offered by your company.

What if you don't have a company pension or retirement plan? Self-employed people can use so-called SEPs (Simplified Employee Pensions) that allow you to defer taxes on 13% of net business income, up to $22,500. A business owner can set up a Keogh plan. The three types are defined-benefit, profit-sharing and money-purchase. Depending on which you choose, you annually are allowed to contribute as little as you can afford or as much as $120,000. And don't overlook the merits of the humble IRA (Individual Retirement Account). Even though Congress has limited the deductibility of IRA deposits, you can still write off some or all of your contribution if you're not covered by a retirement plan at work or if you're married and have an adjusted gross income below $40,000 ($25,000 for single taxpayers). Even if you can't get an IRA deduction, you could still contribute $2,000 annually ($2,250 for married couples with one working spouse) and watch those earnings grow tax deferred.

## Aim for stocks' higher returns.

The most effective way to build your retirement portfolio is to invest in stocks rather than bonds and cash. Over nearly 70 years, stocks have returned an average of 10% annually, twice the 5% return for Treasury bonds. Cash investments such as Treasury bills merely matched the inflation rate at around 3%. To diversify properly, buy a variety of stocks and stock funds including blue chips for relatively stable returns and small companies for zippy gains that have averaged 12% annually over time. For even more variety, spice up your mix with overseas stocks and funds.

# 2

# Invest Wisely for Every Life Stage

Even a generous company pension and savings plan, coupled with the maximum Social Security benefit, probably won't provide you with enough income for a completely carefree retirement. To keep your standard of living from dropping dramatically after you leave work, you must buttress your retirement savings with your own investments. And you can't just sock your money away. You have to take time to invest it regularly and wisely regardless of which life stage you have reached. Let's assume, for example, that you had the discipline to save $500 a month for 30 years and stashed it all in a riskless money-market fund. If your money earned 6.5% annually, on average, you would have accumulated about $553,000. Now let's say that you put your money instead into a growth-minded mix of mostly stocks and some bonds (or mutual funds that invest in these securities). Assuming an average return approaching 10% a year, an achievable one for such a portfolio over three decades, you would have ended up with a cool $1 million bundle. The price for nearly doubling your return, however, is much greater uncertainty in the short run.With only a moderately risky growth portfolio, you still should be prepared to ride out market drops that could be as grim as 20% in the course of several months or even weeks.

Are you game? If so, you should be able to put any reasonable retirement dream within reach by following the investing strategies outlined in this chapter. Whether you are starting or unscrambling your nest egg, the key decisions in the years ahead will hinge mainly on how old you are, where your financial assets currently are concentrated, your outlook for the economy and—most important—your tolerance for risk. The prevailing moods of the stock and bond markets are just two of the factors you must weigh in deploying your money. You should also make gradual adjustments in your mix of assets to correspond with your changing needs for capital growth, steady income or a combination of the two, particularly as you draw nearer to the day when you call it a career.

## Zero in on Your Comfort Zone

Regardless of your age or how well you have diversified your portfolio, the most important challenge is to find your comfort zone and to know that it will change as your temples gray and your career progresses. Astute asset allocation begins with a careful analysis of your investments and other aspects of your financial life to determine how each of these affects your exposure to the following types of risk.

♦ **Inflation risk.** Rising prices will reduce the purchasing power of an investment. An annual inflation rate of 5% over 15 years will cut the value of $1,000 to $480. Overcautious investors who hoard assets in low-yielding investments such as savings accounts and money-market funds may not earn enough to outpace rising prices. Rising inflation also erodes the value of future income generated by investments with fixed payments, most notably long-term bonds.

♦ **Interest-rate risk.** Rising interest rates will cause investments to drop in price. Higher rates make yields on existing bonds less attractive, so their market values decline. Rising rates also hurt stocks by making their dividend yields less appealing. People who invest borrowed money through margin accounts or have other types of floating-rate debt increase their risk because higher interest rates cut into their net profits.

♦ **Economic risk.** Slower growth in the economy will cause investments to fall in price. Shares of small growth companies may shrink because they require a booming economy to sustain their robust earnings gains. Cyclical companies, such as automakers and chemical producers, can't easily cut their hefty fixed costs during a recession. So their earnings and share prices may well nosedive. Economic downturns can also undercut junk bonds issued by financially weak firms that might default.

♦ **Market risk.** This includes such factors as political developments and Wall Street fads that can batter investment markets. Tax law changes, trade agreements, program trading and the quirks of investor psychology all contribute to market risk, which has accounted for much of the stock market's day-to-day volatility. Gold also carries considerable market risk because its price moves sharply when political or military upheavals in other countries encourage the flight of capital.

♦ **Specific risk.** This covers occurrences that may affect only a particular company or industry. Poor management or bad luck can dampen earnings or even bankrupt a company. And high-flying growth stocks are particularly vulnerable to earnings disappointments. Individuals take on a high degree of specific risk when they buy stock in a firm with a heavy debt burden or invest in specialty stock funds, often called sector funds because they concentrate their holdings in a single industry such as energy. Specific risk also includes the chance that government regulation will harm a particular group of companies.

 **Take an Inventory of Your Assets**

After uncovering the major risks in your portfolio, you can redeploy assets to reduce your exposure. Don't limit your inventory to investments that are kept in a brokerage account. Your earning power probably is by far your most valuable asset; equity in a home may come next. Many investors also have substantial assets invested in company pension plans or insurance policies with significant cash values. And entrepreneurs should take a close reading of the risks that threaten the value of their small business.

Risk tends to creep up on even vigilant investors. Your holdings in a retirement plan may grow more quickly than you realize, particularly if you make regular contributions or reinvest your returns. But with this success comes a problem. Growth in one asset can throw a portfolio out of balance if other investments don't keep up. If a prolonged bull market boosts the value of your stockholdings, you may need to sell some shares to restore the balance between stocks and other assets. Similarly, when a single stock does extremely well, you have to consider whether it's time to shed some shares. Be especially wary of loading up on your company's stock through retirement and savings plans. If the company runs into trouble, both your job and your stock could be endangered at the same time. If you live in a one-company town, the value of your home may also be tied to the fortunes of that firm. To gauge your own situation, you will need to conduct a survey of your investments and other aspects of your finances. Here's a rundown of the strengths and weaknesses of various assets.

**Stocks and stock funds.** They are vulnerable to the possibility that skittish investors will panic for some reason and drive share prices down en masse (an example of market risk). But risks related to inflation, interest rates or economic growth may vary considerably from stock to stock. For example, a sharp increase in the inflation rate depresses stock prices because it may reduce the purchasing power of future dividends to shareholders. What's more, inflation generally coincides with higher interest rates, which draw investors from stocks to bonds. Because firms such as retailers, consumer product manufacturers and service companies can pass along cost increases to customers relatively easily, they are more likely to prosper during periods of high inflation.

Slowing economic growth hurts some firms more than others. Manufacturers with high overhead, known as cyclicals, cannot easily cut costs when a recession slices sales, so their earnings quickly tail off. Many small growth companies also require an expanding economy to sustain their earnings growth and stock prices. By contrast, firms that sell necessities such as food or clothing often shine even in a lackluster economy, and their shares tend to hold up relatively well. Since overseas stocks are partly immune to changes in the American economy and markets, they may stand firm while U.S. stocks sink. Unlike domestic issues, however, foreign shares carry currency risk. A weaker dollar abroad helps to inflate returns that are earned on overseas assets, while a stronger dollar deflates them.

**Bonds and bond funds.** Their prices fall when interest rates rise. But the extent of the drop depends on a bond's maturity and the amount of its coupon. Short-term bonds fall slightly when interest rates move upward, and a high coupon also offers some protection against climbing rates. At the opposite extreme, zero-coupon bonds fall sharply when rates head higher. A recession generally brings lower interest rates, which boost bond prices. But some issues react negatively to the threat of an economic slowdown. So-called junk bonds, in particular, may lose ground because investors fear that financially weak firms will default and fail to make payments of interest and principal to bondholders on time. U.S. Treasury and high-grade corporate bonds gain the most during hard times because income investors seek them out as safe havens.

**Real estate investments.** Although they tend to keep pace with inflation over time, they present other hazards. If you own a rental property, you run the risk that you won't find a tenant. A real estate partnership that owns several properties in different regions can reduce such risks through diversification, but it may lose value if tax changes or a recession drive down property values across the country. Real estate investment trusts, called REITs, and the funds that own them, can fluctuate with the stock market as well as with property values.

**Gold and other hard assets.** The price of gold can skyrocket when the inflation rate rises rapidly. Between 1968 and 1988, the consumer price index posted nine annual spurts of 6% or more. During those years, gold rewarded investors with an average gain of 34%. Gold-mining stocks are more volatile than the metal itself. Other tangible assets present their own problems. While paintings, antique furniture or rare stamps may outpace inflation in the long run, prices of items such as baseball cards are largely subject to collectors' whims.

## Achieve the Best Blend for You

Why does asset allocation determine most of an investor's return? According to researchers, the basic reason is that different types of investments don't rise and fall at the same time. By diversifying among stocks, bonds or cash, you can usually offset losses in one asset category with gains in another. For example, in October 1987, when stocks plummeted nearly 22%, long-term bonds rose 6%. The opposite proved true in 1994. Bonds tumbled 3%, while the S&P 500 eked out a 1% gain. While diversification can't guarantee that you'll never lose money, it can reduce your portfolio's overall risk and dramatically improve your odds of reaching your investment goals.

To determine the most efficient mix of investments for a retirement portfolio, experts first look at the correlation between various asset classes. Correlation is the technical term for comparing how different assets perform relative to one another over varying market cycles. The analysts measure correlation on a scale of 1.0 (two assets move precisely in tandem over time) to -1.0 (the investments always move in opposite directions). You ideally want to build a portfolio of different types of assets that are not closely correlated to one another.

That way, you won't get clobbered by all your investments dropping in value at roughly the same time.

What's more, a properly diversified portfolio lets you put some of your money in potentially high-paying assets that otherwise might be too risky. You perform this alchemy by combining them with investments to which the high fliers are only weakly correlated. For example, a portfolio entirely invested in the large domestic stocks that make up the S&P 500 would have gained over 14% a year during the past two decades. But you could have earned 16% a year over the same time with a portfolio invested 65% in S&P 500 stocks, 20% in overseas stocks (with a 0.5 correlation to U.S. blue chips) and 15% in small-company shares (a 0.8 correlation to the S&P 500). In allocating assets, the pros rely not only on stocks' and bonds' past performance but also on estimates of their potential future returns. These predictions are based on forecasts of how market cycles will affect the performance of different asset classes. The model portfolios in this chapter are based on projections that over the next 10 years or so large-company stocks will climb an average of 12% annually, bonds will rise 5% a year and cash investments such as Treasury bills will edge up almost 4% annually.

 ## Retirement Portfolios for Life's Stages

As you grow older, start a family and move closer to retirement, your investment goals and taste for risk change. Your portfolio should change along with you. Younger people, for example, can afford to aim for high returns with aggressive portfolios because they have many years to recover from market slumps. But as you get closer to retirement, you need to shift to a more cautious allocation that will preserve your gains. There's a second, equally powerful argument in favor of asset allocation. Academic studies show that about 90% of investors' returns come from the right combination of assets, with the remainder derived from their skill in picking securities and from timely trading. To help you design your own allocation, MONEY surveyed many experts to devise a model portfolio for each of the four major stages in most people's working lives—starting out, raising a family, peak earning years and retirement living (the portfolios are depicted on pages 26 to 29).

## Aiming high in your 20s to early 30s.
You now have about 30 years before early retirement. So you can afford to gun for growth by stashing at least 75% of your portfolio in stocks and stock funds. Go for as much as 100% if you feel comfortable riding out market swings. Those who tend to get queasy in roller-coaster markets might put as much as 25% of their money in bonds and bond funds, which pay interest that will help stabilize their portfolios. Based on past performance, this 75-25 lineup has the potential to return over 9% annually.

For beginners with small savings, a single fund that buys large-company stocks is a sound choice. Blue chips tend to offer solid capital appreciation with less volatility than smaller stocks. Nervous investors might want to opt for a balanced or asset-allocation fund instead. These all-in-one portfolios typically keep about 60% of their assets in stocks and the rest in risk-cushioning bonds and other fixed-income investments. Investors who have $10,000 or more ought to assemble a diversified portfolio of funds. Allocate about 30% of your assets to large-company stocks, 25% to small-company stocks (those with annual revenues of $500 million or less) and 20% to overseas stocks. Small stocks historically have outpaced their bigger brothers, though with greater volatility. Overseas stocks can spice up your portfolio because many foreign economies, particularly developing ones in Asia and Latin America, are likely to grow much faster than ours over the next decade. The risks you face are political instability and adverse swings in the value of the dollar. But if you can hold on through the downturns, your retirement fund could benefit greatly in the long run.

For a smoother ride to those higher returns, you might include both value and growth-stock funds in your port-

# Starting Out

Single person, late twenties, with $10,000 saved

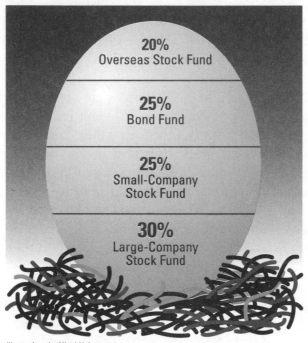

**20%**
Overseas Stock Fund

**25%**
Bond Fund

**25%**
Small-Company
Stock Fund

**30%**
Large-Company
Stock Fund

Illustrations by Nigel Holmes

folio. Value managers look for out-of-favor companies with share prices that do not fully reflect their earnings prospects or asset values. By contrast, growth-stock managers, as the name suggests, prefer companies with rapidly accelerating revenues and earnings, even though their shares typically will command premium prices. You can't really predict which investing style will be more successful in any given year. Studies show that over periods of 20 years or more, however, value has a slight performance advantage over growth.

As for your fixed-income holdings, put about 15% of your money in investment-grade bonds with intermediate maturities of five to 10 years. Studies show that five-

## Raising a Family

Couple, thirties, two preschoolers, $50,000 saved

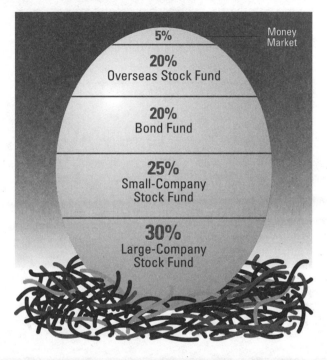

5%  Money Market

20%
Overseas Stock Fund

20%
Bond Fund

25%
Small-Company
Stock Fund

30%
Large-Company
Stock Fund

year issues produce 96% of the return of 30-year issues with only half the volatility. About 5% of your money should go into a convertible bond fund, which will give you a shot at capital gains, or to a high-yield fund, which takes on extra risk in pursuit of the fatter yields paid by junk bonds. But steer clear of bond funds that carry sales charges or fees that total more than 1% of net assets. Their managers generally can't overcome these high expenses with superior performance. (Fees are listed in a fund's prospectus.)

### Family planning in your early 30s to 40s. With young families to provide for and mortgages to pay off,

# Prime Earning Years

Couple, early fifties, three teens, $200,000 saved

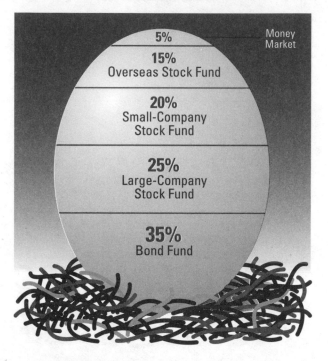

5% — Money Market

15%
Overseas Stock Fund

20%
Small-Company
Stock Fund

25%
Large-Company
Stock Fund

35%
Bond Fund

many investors in this age group prefer to reduce their portfolios' risk level. Just don't overdo it. You will be working for another 20 years or more, so you should keep at least 75% of your money in stocks. You can achieve that balance by gradually trimming back your stock funds and moving the excess cash to a money-market fund. Overall, our model is designed to give you average returns of about 8.75% annually. At this stage, you should further diversify your bond holdings. High earners should consider transferring the money in their convertible or high-yield corporate bond fund to a tax-free municipal bond fund and adding enough money so that it becomes 10% of the portfolio. A taxable alterna-

# Retirement Living

Couple, mid sixties, empty nesters, $400,000 saved

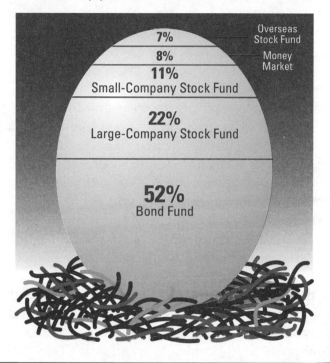

7%
Overseas Stock Fund

8%
Money Market

11%
Small-Company Stock Fund

22%
Large-Company Stock Fund

52%
Bond Fund

tive is an international bond fund. Fixed-income markets in the U.S. and abroad generally move in different directions, so you will offset a falling market with one that is on the rise. Foreign bond funds, of course, can respond sharply to currency fluctuations. In the last quarter of 1992, for example, the typical international bond fund lost 1.5% of its value when Europe's exchange-rate agreement collapsed. But if you can let your money ride for at least 10 years, the swings will likely even out.

## Hitting stride in your early 40s to 50s. You have
reached your peak earning years—just in time to pay your kids' college bills. Don't let that serve as an excuse

to neglect your savings. Stocks should still be the center-piece of your portfolio. But ease back on risk by reduc-ing your exposure to large-company stocks to 25%, small caps to 20% and overseas stocks to 15%. This model aims to provide you with average returns of around 8% annually. You can add greater stability to your portfolio by emphasizing value funds. Since value funds focus on bargain-priced companies, they tend to fall less far than their high-flying growth peers during market corrections. And the stocks in value funds tend to pay dividends that will bolster your returns in down years. In the fixed-income portion of your portfolio, you might seek addi-tional security by cutting international bonds to 5% and exchanging your intermediate-term corporate bond fund for one that holds government issues. Investors in the 28% bracket or above, however, will probably do better with tax-exempt bonds. To earn high returns with mini-mum risk, look for muni funds with annual fees of less than 1% that hold mainly bonds rated A or higher.

**Kicking back in your early 50s to 60s.** With retirement around the corner, you may be tempted to cash in your stock funds and tuck the proceeds into principal-preserving bond funds or bank CDs. That could prove to be a bad move. At 50 you still have a lifetime of at least 30 years ahead of you. If inflation stays at 3% a year, that will cut the purchasing power of today's dollar in half in only 12 years. Thus you should still hold a roughly 50% stake in stocks. Such a model portfolio should produce average returns of around 7.5% a year. In addition, now is an excellent time to move out of international bonds entirely and into U.S. Government issues for greater safety. Truly risk-averse investors might anchor their portfolios with Treasury notes, which mature in two to 10 years, because their principal and interest payments are federally guaranteed. You can opt for a Treasury-only bond fund. But odds are you can do just as well purchasing the Treasuries directly with no fee from your nearest Federal Reserve bank or branch. And that's a good deal for investors in any stage of life.

# 3

# Call It Quits Earlier With Confidence

Most people, regardless of their age or career path, like to muse about retiring early and making leisure their primary pursuit. Yet more and more Americans are actually achieving that lofty goal. In fact, as life expectancy has risen, the age at which people retire has declined. The average age of retirement recently was around 61, down from 65 in 1970. Millions of wage slaves now are declaring their independence in their fifties and even forties. For them, retirement has come to mean almost anything except shuffling off to play another round of shuffleboard. Today's youthful retirees often run part-time businesses, volunteer at nonprofit institutions, take their hobbies seriously and travel the globe.

You probably have thought about how you would spend the time you earned after retiring early. Whatever your dream, the chances of attaining it are far better than you might imagine. Financial lures abound for people who cut loose while still young. A survey of large employers by the Wyatt Co., a benefits consulting firm, shows that 93% paid pensions to retirees at age 55 or earlier if they had served at least a specified number of years, usually 10 or 15. More people are eligible to receive pensions as a result of federal legislation that requires companies to cut vesting time from 10 years to either five or seven. Popular savings programs like 401(k)s and IRAs offer ways to build cash for an early retirement. And Social Security benefits may not be substantially reduced if you stop working before 62, the age when you can start getting the government checks.

Early retirement is not for everyone, of course. Many can't afford it. In one MONEY survey, having enough money for retirement was the No. 1 financial worry for people 35 to 49. You might not be able to get out early if you are facing tuition bills for your children's education well into your fifties. Your pension may be inadequate (or nonexistent) if you hopped jobs or work for a small firm. Others are psychologically unprepared for early retirement. You may not be ready either to give up the camaraderie of business associates or to spend a lot more time with your mate. One spouse may want to retire early but the other doesn't. More often, this scenario involves a woman who wants to stay on because she entered or re-entered the work force late or only recently landed a challenging job. Fear of boredom is genuine for those who can't figure out how they would occupy days without deadlines.

## Traits for aspiring early retirees. For those

intrigued by the concept of early retirement, the main prerequisites are preparation, creativity and dedication. You will have to reposition your investments while working to amass the pot needed at the retirement age you select. Quitting early obviously means that your savings must last longer than otherwise. Assuming a modest 4% annual return adjusted for inflation, someone planning to retire at 55 has to sock away $560,000 to collect $30,000 a year until age 90, compared with $468,000 for someone waiting until he is 65. The younger retiree also has 10 fewer years to accumulate that 20% additional cash reserve. Shrewd investing alone will not swing early retirement for everyone. There may well be some necessary trade-offs to weigh in the future, like telling your kids to set their sights on first-rate public colleges rather than expensive private schools. And you may have to make small sacrifices, such as cutting back on luxuries or entertainment, either before or after you retire.

The more creative you are earlier, the less spartan you will have to be later. Try to devise ways of building your own retirement annuity, not through an insurance company but through your own skills. Be sure to ask yourself the following question. What could I do now that will bring in steady annual income after I retire? The answer might be honing a hobby that you will turn into a sideline business in retirement. It might be buying rental real estate today with a mortgage you will have paid off by the time you retire, thus positioning you to earn a tidy, positive cash flow. Or it might be picking up a new skill that you have long coveted.

The expertise that you gain could eventually become rewarding in all respects. But consulting, the most popular form of post-retirement entrepreneurism, ideally requires building contacts and a reputation before stepping down from your current job. Trying to market yourself as a consultant after you quit working can end up taking more time than you spent at your old job. If your dream involves running your own business, you had better get started now. Many service companies operate during nights and weekends and require no more start-up capital than the cost of a personal computer, laser printer, fax and telephone answering machine. Even if you are not contemplating a second career, you should start gearing up today to make sure you have enough money to carry you through retirement.

**What you'll need to set aside.** Deciding to retire early demands the right temperament as well as enough money. To help you gauge the former, take the quiz "Are You Really Ready to Retire?" later in this chapter. After all, a lot of people say that they expect to retire between the ages of 50 and 64. If so, they will likely live another 18 to 29 years on average. The most content early retirees are people who developed outside interests while working. Their identities were not wedded to their careers. If you can't come up with at least a dozen things you like to do, you're probably not a good candidate for early retirement. You must also determine whether you can swing it financially. For estimates of the costs and savings that are involved, fill out the worksheets beginning on pages 44 and 46.

Expect that your post-career expenses will equal 70% to 80% of your pre-retirement income. Next, figure how much you can safely expect from Social Security and your company pension. Social Security now replaces about a third of pre-retirement income, with the percentage falling as your salary climbs above $35,000. About 60% of retirees get pensions, which typically are based on your years of service and your salary for the last five years on the job. Ask your benefits department for an estimate of the pension you can expect at age 55 and at your company's normal retirement age, usually 65. Some employers will also calculate your pension starting on the date you hope to leave work.

Even though your pension check will almost always increase the longer you work, leaving your job before 65 may not cost as much as you think. Some experts argue that working past 60 can actually cut the total value of your future benefits in current dollars. Pension formulas typically increase your annual benefit more slowly after age 60. As a result, the only financial benefit you might receive from working an extra year would be that year's salary. Ask your benefits department what your pension will be if you leave at various ages, both on an annual basis and as a lump sum. Then have your accountant figure out when your pension will stop growing enough to make working longer worthwhile.

In recent years, many companies have offered special early retirement packages that sweeten pensions for employees who volunteer to accept these offers. Some of these deals are worth grabbing, but others are strikingly stingy. (We provide guidance on evaluating such arrangements later in this chapter.) Note, however, that an often overlooked pension penalty, introduced into tax law in the 1980s, may have the effect of discouraging some high earners from retiring early. Anyone retiring at 55 cannot collect more than a maximum annual pension benefit (the amount varies with your salary scale). This ceiling rises for people who retire at age 62 and those taking pensions starting at 65. Consult with your accountant or financial planner. Many companies may be able

# Are You Really Ready To Retire?

While you may be all set for a financially secure retirement, you may not realize how much life after work can draw on your emotional reserves. If you suddenly find yourself with 40 or more hours a week of free time that you haven't adequately prepared for, you could be headed for trouble. These questions, based on the findings of gerontologists and psychologists, will help you determine how well prepared you are for the day when the alarm clock no longer rules. Answer each question that applies to you. Then tally the points assigned to each answer for your score. At the end, you can see what the specialists think.

|  | YES | NO |
|---|---|---|
| ✦ Will you be able to cut back your hours at work gradually instead of all at once? <br> *Change may exact a toll if it's too abrupt. Making the transition slowly gives you time to adjust at your own pace.* | +3 | -3 |
| ✦ Are you married? <br> *Being unmarried can reduce an individual's life expectancy more than smoking or being overweight.* | +4 | -4 |
| ✦ If you're married, is the relationship satisfying? <br> *Retirement can put a strain on your marriage. If you don't get along before you retire, chances are things will get worse afterward.* | +2 | -2 |
| ✦ If your spouse is working, will he or she retire at about the same time as you? <br> *An increasingly common problem occurs when the husband retires while his younger wife continues to work; it often reduces his self-esteem and creates confusion about household duties.* | +3 | -3 |
| ✦ If you're not married, do you live with someone? <br> *Although being in a satisfying marriage is the best way to overcome feelings of isolation, living with someone is a close second.* | +3 | -3 |
| ✦ If you live alone, do you have daily contact with family or friends? <br> *This is another substitute for a live-in companion.* | +2 | -2 |
| ✦ Do you have at least one person outside of the office (for example, your spouse, a friend, even your banker or broker) in whom you can easily and comfortably confide? <br> *Even if you rarely share intimacies with your pals, just the presence of a confidant can often be crucial to keeping your peace of mind.* | +4 | -4 |

- ✦ Do you have a place at home or outside of it where you can have total privacy?     +2   -2
  *Together is fine up to a point. Everybody needs a retreat.*

- ✦ Do you try not to hang around the office after the workday is over?     +3   -3
  *If you're spending too many hours at work, you may be dependent on the job for social life. Letting go will be hard for you.*

- ✦ Have you made any new friends outside of work this year?     +3   -3
  *Don't make the mistake of assuming your work colleagues will still have time for you after you retire.*

- ✦ Are you involved with community, church or cultural groups?     +4   -4
  *Such activities may prove to be the center of your post-work days. Don't wait until retirement to get involved outside your job.*

- ✦ Do you schedule activities such as fishing trips, museum visits and picnics to fill up your free time?     +3   -3
  *Retirement may well be the first time in 40 years that you will control your own time. You should know how to plan your days without a boss looking over your shoulder.*

- ✦ Have you taken part in an intellectual pursuit, such as attending a class or lecture, or a physical one, such as a competitive sport, in the past month?     +2   -2
  *Aim for a variety of activities. Just because you like fishing doesn't mean that after retirement you will enjoy it every day.*

- ✦ Have you learned something new (say, a foreign language or computer skills) in the past five years?     +2   -2
  *Taking on new challenges shows an openness to change.*

- ✦ Were you able to adjust easily when your children left home or during other periods of major change?     +4   -4
  *If you have been able to weather most of life's changes, you'll almost surely adjust well to retirement.*

- ✦ Are you looking forward to retirement?     +3   -3
  *Your attitude can cast a shadow over everything. A negative one could become a self-fulfilling prophecy.*

If you score 18 points or above, you are on solid footing. Between zero and 18, you have some catching up to do. Below zero, you need to work hard on improving your emotional preparation for retiring.

to skirt these ceilings by paying any higher obligations out of the company's reserves rather than pensions.

**How to overhaul your portfolio.** In your twenties and thirties, stocks or stock funds should make up as much as 70% to 80% of your retirement savings, with the balance in bond investments. As you approach early retirement you will want to start gradually reducing the stock portion until it hits a still sizable 50% when you quit. Why? With inflation and the long life expectancy of retirees, you need growth in your portfolio. Given steep top tax brackets of 36% and 39.6%, choosing the most tax-advantaged and cost-efficient vehicles for your retirement needs will also help your nest egg grow faster. Someone setting aside $4,000 a year for 35 years in a 401(k) plan earning an average of 8% annually will have $744,400 at retirement, compared with only $301,000 if he or she had put the same amount in taxable investments.

**Why company plans are crucial.** With capital gains taxed at 28%, upper-income investors with portfolios outside their sheltered retirement plans might put income-oriented investments into the plans and keep stocks that produce only capital gains outside. But your first retirement savings dollars should go into workplace plans such as 401(k)s. Yearly contributions of up to $9,500 (the maximum amount rises annually with inflation) are automatically taken out of your paycheck in pretax dollars, giving you the discipline of enforced savings and a tax cutter at the same time. Better yet, most companies that currently are offering 401(k)s match part of your contribution, producing an instant gain. If you work for a nonprofit organization or a school, your employer may offer a 403(b) plan or a tax-sheltered annuity in which you can stash cash.

You can shelter much more if you are self-employed. Some sole proprietors find a SEP (Simplified Employee Pension) is the solution. The maximum contribution is 13% of net business income, or $22,500, whichever is less. A business owner who's nearing retirement can sock away the most by way of a special defined-benefit Keogh that can be funded with contributions totaling up to $120,000 roughly. A small-business owner setting up a plan for employees as well may want to opt for a profit-sharing Keogh, whose annual contribution limit for the business owner is the same as a SEP's. The employer contributes to employees' accounts according to a formula based on their income. A profit-sharing Keogh is more flexible than a SEP, enabling you to vary contributions to employee accounts using such factors as age or length of service. If you want to invest even more for retirement for you and your staff, combine a profit-sharing Keogh with a money-purchase Keogh and put away an additional 7% of net earnings. But you'll have to commit to a set contribution level every year.

## Don't forget IRAs and annuities.
Since the demise of full deductibility for IRA contributions, these accounts have been overlooked by many investors. Yet IRAs should still be the second place for your retirement savings after company plans. You will qualify for a full or a partial IRA deduction if you don't have a company pension or if your adjusted gross income falls below $40,000 for a married couple or $25,000 for singles. Even if you don't get the write-off, you can still put up to $2,000 into a nondeductible IRA every year and get tax-deferred earnings. You should be forewarned, however, that there are paperwork hassles with nondeductible accounts. The solution is to hold deductible and nondeductible IRAs in separate accounts.

Variable and fixed annuities are also marketed as retirement vehicles because their investment earnings are tax deferred too. Variable ones let you put money into portfolios of stocks, bonds or cash. Fixed annuities pay a flat rate of interest. But unless you've already fully funded your workplace plans and IRA and are sure you will stay invested at least 10 years, think twice before putting money into annuities. First, you must put in after-tax dollars. You also could be clobbered by surrender fees of as much as 8% of the amount you withdraw if you take money out within the first eight years, not to mention a 10% tax penalty on your accrued earnings if you want out before age 59.5.

**The pain of future medical bills.** Expenses that are related to health care are likely to consume 15% to 20% of your income in retirement. To ease the burden, you should try to obtain comprehensive health insurance that will cover you from the day you retire until you turn 65 and qualify for Medicare. If you're among the most fortunate early retirees, your employer will let you keep your current coverage. Or, under the federal COBRA law, you can buy medical coverage through your company's group policy for 18 months at your employer's cost. Before your coverage runs out, look into joining your local HMO if it has a so-called open enrollment period (typically one month each year when it must accept all applicants). Also look for affordable private coverage, which is often cheaper than Blue Cross/Blue Shield if you're in good health.

**Some good news on Social Security.** It's a better deal for early retirees than you might expect. True, your checks at 62 could be 20% smaller than if you waited to start receiving them at age 65. But a closer look at the numbers shows that the government actually promotes early retirement when computing Social Security benefits. Consider a 55-year-old male manager with a typical earnings history. If he retires now, in seven years he will begin getting a Social Security benefit of about $845 a month, in today's dollars. If he keeps working until 62, his monthly benefit will amount to about $900, only 7% more. Thus, if this man works seven more years, his extra payoff from Social Security will be peanuts.

The outlook for early retirement in the future is partly cloudy. Since a company plan will typically freeze your pension amount from the time you leave until its regular retirement date, inflation will melt a portion of your benefits. The aging of the U.S. population will also bring with it some ominous thunder for younger members of today's work force. The ratio of employees to retirees at many major corporations has slipped from about 15 to 1 in the 1970s to around 4 to 1 lately. That means as the baby-boom generation nears retirement at the turn of the century, companies will need to hang on to more employees. Early retirement packages may be curtailed lest businesses end up paying retirees almost as much as their employees. Moreover, Congress has approved changes that will snip Social Security benefits for early retirees in the next century. But by then, nearly a generation of Americans will have struggled through-out their youth for a chance to tell their boss to take the dumb job and shove it. Their reward will be an enticing opportunity to spend a full, idyllic third of their lives in well-plotted leisure. And that pleasure is something no government check can match.

##  Figuring How Much You Will Need

You know you must save regularly and invest wisely to have enough money for a worry-free retirement, particu-larly an early one. But how much is enough? Well, let's assume that you will have a pension and Social Security. But those checks most likely will replace less than half your pre-retirement income. For investments to make up the difference of, say, another $20,000 a year that in-creases annually with inflation you would need to retire with a $310,000 portfolio earning 8% pretax.

Instead of panicking about falling short or having to catch up, think instead about how your life will change when you leave work and then estimate the cost of that lifestyle. The traditional rule of thumb that retirees need 80% of their pre-retirement income may not hold true for you. You might consider it a hardship to have to make do with less just when you have time to enjoy the fruits of years of work and savings. Some frugal people may find that they need no more than 50% of their pre-retirement income. Health care aside, Americans over 65 spend 25% to 40% less than younger people do on food, clothing, housing, transportation and other everyday expenses. Whether to aim for 50% or 120% of your pre-retirement income depends on when you plan to stop working and how well you hope to live. Do you envision an early retirement of two homes and country clubs? Or quieter years making do with one car and fewer dinners out? Moreover, with retirement possibly lasting as long as 30 years, don't forget that your living costs will diminish as you age. Expenses tend to be highest for early retirees who travel extensively. Older ones typically spend less on such discretionary items as well as necessities (with the exception of health care).

**These worksheets aren't a chore.** To find out the dollars and cents of retirement, start with the worksheet "Estimate Your Future Costs Now" on page 44. Then let the worksheet titled "How Much You Must Sock Away" on page 46 guide you to an annual savings goal based on your anticipated retirement lifestyle, your current savings and your expected pension and Social Security benefit. For example, housing (line 1 in the worksheet "Estimate Your Future Costs Now") will continue to be your biggest expense even if you don't have a mortgage to pay now. Figure that your property taxes, homeowners insurance, utilities and upkeep will cost you no less than they do now unless you move to a smaller house or to a lower-cost area.

Your food costs (line 3) may decline 25% or so in retirement if you eat out less (obviously you won't buy lunch at work anymore). Transportation costs (line 4) will drop because you will no longer incur commuting expenses. And you may find that you don't need to replace a car so often or even keep two, especially later on. Unless your job never required pricey suits or dresses, you can expect to shave 20% to 35% off clothing costs (line 2). How much travel and entertainment costs (line 12) may change depends on your tastes. If early retirement means that you'll be going on more long trips, be sure to budget for them, since travel is often such retirees' single biggest new expense.

Chances are (you hope) you will have finished paying for your children's education by the time you retire. But think about whether you want to take courses yourself (line 7). You may also want to help your grown children buy a home or pay for their children's schooling. Members of the so-called sandwich generation may have to budget money for the care of their aging parents (line 16). As for loan payments (line 10), you should strive to reduce credit-card balances and other debt while you are still working.

Life insurance costs (line 8) usually go down or, in the case of disability insurance, disappear in retirement, since you typically will no longer have earnings from work to protect. Your income from investments, including those in retirement plans, doesn't need to be safeguarded by life insurance. Nor does your pension plan because federal law requires that a surviving spouse be paid a reduced benefit—unless he or she has formally waived it. On the other hand, you may decide that you need life insurance to provide liquidity in your estate or supplement a small pension for a surviving spouse.

Your biggest savings on taxes (line 15), assuming that you don't work in retirement, will be the Social Security and Medicare tax on wages. In addition, some states exempt some income from Social Security benefits and pensions from taxes. But don't look for many other breaks. Under the new federal tax law, as much as 85% of your Social Security benefits may be taxable, depending on your overall income.

Trying to predict medical expenses (line 9) is tough because you don't know what health problems you may face or the outcome of the health reform debate. Nonetheless, for purposes of the worksheet, assume that health care costs could be higher. In addition, early retirees may face higher medical costs until they qualify for Medicare at 65 if they have to buy their own insurance, which can cost up to $5,000 a year. You also should figure on your health costs staying high after 65 because of higher out-of-pocket medical expenses and insurance premiums. For example, a supplemental Medicare policy could run as

# Estimate Your Future Costs Now

**♦ Line 1:** If you pay off your mortgage and take care of all necessary maintenance problems before you retire, housing costs should drop by as much as 25% to 30%. Count on even more shrinkage if you sell your house and buy a smaller one. Condominium owners and renters should factor in the expense of periodic maintenance and rent increases. And anyone who plans to spend more time at home should anticipate paying higher utilities charges.

**♦ Line 2:** Financial planners estimate that if you are moving from business suits to jeans, you can expect to reduce clothing expenses by 20% to 35%.

**♦ Line 4:** Scratch commuting costs. Other transportation expenses will increase if you intend to be very active. Planners recommend that two-car couples keep both autos during retirement, especially if both are fairly active.

**♦ Line 6:** Most people keep giving the same amounts to charitable, political and educational institutions, as well as to family members outside the immediate household. But the overall figure drops, usually by the amount you used to give at the office.

**♦ Line 7:** If your kids will be grown by the time you retire, you can eliminate education expenses, unless you plan to help pay your grandchildren's college bills. And if you intend to return to school yourself, check into reduced tuition costs for senior citizens.

**♦ Line 8:** There will be little change in your payout for property, personal liability and automobile insurance. But retirees can generally reduce their life insurance coverage by at least 50% or, if their spouses are fully provided for under their pension plan, eliminate the policy altogether.

**♦ Line 9:** If you are currently covered by a company health plan, expect medical and dental costs to spurt by about 50% because of increased illnesses combined with reduced insurance coverage. Medicare pays part of doctors' fees and hospital bills. Check your company's coverage for retirees.

**♦ Line 10:** Most retirement experts say you should plan to be debt-free by the time you retire, thereby eliminating loan repayment expenses.

**♦ Line 12:** How much you continue to spend for entertainment depends on how active you are. Expect such expenditures to rise an average of about 20% during your retirement.

**♦ Line 13:** You probably should be prepared to budget for higher veterinary bills if you will have an aging dog, cat or other pet.

**♦ Line 14:** While your contributions to savings and pension plans cease at retirement, many financial planners encourage clients to continue setting aside about 10% of their income as a hedge against a sudden spurt in inflation.

**♦ Line 15:** If you don't work, it's farewell to Social Security (FICA) taxes. Also check laws in your state because some don't tax income from retirement plans. The conventional wisdom that you will be in a lower tax bracket after retirement is no longer true for high earners. You will be taxed on up to 50% of your Social Security benefits if the total of your adjusted gross income, nontaxable interest, and half your Social Security benefits exceeds $25,000 ($32,000 if you are married). If that total is over $34,000 ($44,000 for married couples), you'll owe tax on up to 85% of Social Security benefits.

**♦ Line 16:** With more and more adult children now expecting some form of financial help from Mom and Dad, plus Americans' increasing average longevity, you could be contributing to the down payment on a child's first house while paying for a parent's nursing home.

On the right, the figure that is called total current expenses should equal approximately 100% of your current before-tax income. By dividing your total expenses at retirement by your current gross income, you will arrive at the percentage of your current income that you will need to live comfortably in your retirement years.

| EXPENSES | AT RETIREMENT | CURRENT YEAR |
|---|---|---|
| **1.** Housing. Rent or mortgage payments, property taxes, utilities (gas, oil, electricity and water), telephone, home furnishings, household services, maintenance, improvements | _____ | _____ |
| **2.** Clothing. Purchases and cleaning | _____ | _____ |
| **3.** Food. (including tobacco and alcohol) | _____ | _____ |
| **4.** Transportation. Car repair and maintenance, installment payments, gas, commuting costs, other | _____ | _____ |
| **5.** Gifts. | _____ | _____ |
| **6.** Contributions. | _____ | _____ |
| **7.** Education. | _____ | _____ |
| **8.** Insurance. Life, medical, auto, property, liability | _____ | _____ |
| **9.** Medical and dental care. Premiums, deductible and out-of-pocket costs | _____ | _____ |
| **10.** Loan repayment costs. | _____ | _____ |
| **11.** Personal care. Grooming, health club, other | _____ | _____ |
| **12.** Entertainment. Vacations, dining out, movies, plays, concerts, sports events, cable TV, videocassettes, entertaining, sports, hobbies, other | _____ | _____ |
| **13.** Pet expenses. | _____ | _____ |
| **14.** Investments and retirement savings. Contribution to company plans, IRAs, Keoghs, SEPs and other investments | _____ | _____ |
| **15.** Taxes. Federal, FICA, state, local | _____ | _____ |
| **16.** Support of relatives. | _____ | _____ |
| **Total Expenses.** (add lines 1 through 16) | _____ | _____ |
| **Total Current Expenses Divided by Gross Income.** | _____ | _____ |
| **Total Expenses at Retirement Divided by Gross Income.** | _____ | _____ |

# How Much You Must Sock Away

The worksheet at right will tell you how much you need to start saving now to hold on to your standard of living in retirement. The multipliers that are used in lines 7, 9 and 11 allow for inflation by assuming that your investments will grow at three percentage points over the inflation rate, before and after retirement. This keeps all of the figures in today's dollars.

✦ **Line 3:** You and your spouse can easily keep tabs on what you have coming to you from Social Security. Just call Social Security's toll-free number (800-772-1213) and ask for a copy of its Personal Earnings and Benefits Estimate Statement (PEBES) request form. Two to three weeks after submitting this request form to the agency, you should expect to get a free statement that notes your annual earnings to date and estimates your monthly Social Security benefit if you choose to retire at age 62, 65 or 70. If you should find a mistake in the statement, be prepared to send proof of your earnings to correct it. If you or your spouse are 60 or older, you should have already received the statement, which the agency is supposed to send to folks in the year of their 60th birthday. If not, be sure to call Social Security to find out why.

✦ **Line 4:** Your company benefits department may be able to estimate your pension. Make sure the estimate assumes that you continue working until your retirement age at your current salary. That will understate your likely eventual payout but will keep the figure in today's dollars.

✦ **Line 7:** The multipliers in column A incorporate the cautious assumption that men will live to 90 and women to 94—longer than 85% of them do now. Single men should use the multiplier under "men." Women and married couples should use the one under "women," since wives usually outlive their husbands.

✦ **Line 8:** Your personal retirement portfolio includes any investments that you have specifically earmarked for retirement, aside from your

IRA or Keogh. For your employer-sponsored savings plans, check the most recent statement from your 401(k), profit-sharing, thrift or stock ownership plan and total your vested balance in each.

✦ **Line 12:** You should consult the annual statement from these plans to find and total the amount that your company contributed on your behalf to each of the plans last year. Then enter the total.

| AGE AT WHICH YOU EXPECT TO RETIRE | MULTIPLIER A MEN | MULTIPLIER A WOMEN |
|---|---|---|
| 55 | 22.1 | 23.5 |
| 56 | 21.8 | 23.2 |
| 57 | 21.4 | 22.8 |
| 58 | 21.0 | 22.5 |
| 59 | 20.6 | 22.1 |
| 60 | 20.2 | 21.8 |
| 61 | 19.8 | 21.4 |
| 62 | 19.3 | 21.0 |
| 63 | 18.9 | 20.6 |
| 64 | 18.4 | 20.2 |
| 65 | 17.9 | 19.8 |
| 66 | 17.4 | 19.3 |
| 67 | 16.9 | 18.9 |

| TIME UNTIL YOU EXPECT TO RETIRE | MULTIPLIER B | MULTIPLIER C |
|---|---|---|
| 1 year | 1.03 | 1.000 |
| 3 years | 1.09 | .324 |
| 5 years | 1.16 | .188 |
| 7 years | 1.23 | .131 |
| 9 years | 1.30 | .098 |
| 11 years | 1.38 | .078 |
| 13 years | 1.47 | .064 |
| 15 years | 1.56 | .054 |
| 20 years | 1.81 | .037 |

**1.** Current gross income                                                    _____

**2.** Annual income needed in retirement, in today's dollars
(70% of line 1)                                                                _____

**3.** Annual Social Security retirement benefits                              _____

**4.** Annual pension benefits                                                 _____

**5.** Guaranteed annual retirement income (line 3 plus line 4)               _____

**6.** Additional retirement income needed (line 2 minus line 5)              _____

**7.** Capital required to provide additional retirement income
(line 6 times multiplier from column A at left)                                _____

**8.** Amount you have saved already

_____ + _____ + _____ = _____

   personal          IRA/Keogh          employer-        total savings
   retirement                       sponsored
   portfolio                      savings plans

**9.** What your current investments will have grown to by the time you
retire (total from line 8 times multiplier from column B at left)             _____

**10.** Additional retirement capital required (line 7 minus line 9)          _____

**11.** Total annual savings still needed (line 10 times multiplier,
column C at left)                                                              _____

**12.** Annual employer contributions to your company savings plans           _____

**13.** Amount you need to set aside each year (line 11 minus line 12)        _____ much as $3,500 a year. And don't forget routine dental costs, which may mount with age and are unlikely to be covered by your insurance company.

**Don't expect to stop saving.** That's because saving is one of the only ways you can counteract inflation. Experts recommend that you plan to put aside up to 10% of your income annually in the first few years after you stop working. Moreover, in your early retirement years, you might take a part-time job to supplement your income from pensions and taxable investments. That way your tax-deferred accounts can keep on growing to help cover unexpected costs and provide income when you stop working altogether.

Now fill out the worksheet titled "How Much You Must Sock Away" to determine the amount you should save every year until you finally stop working. As the line-by-line instructions specify, you'll need estimates of your future Social Security benefit and your company pension. If you're close to retirement, your firm's benefits department may be willing to project a pension benefit that has been based on your planned retirement age, which will be more accurate than one based on your current years of service.

You will likely find that your pension and Social Security won't equal your expected retirement living costs. If you retired last year and were earning $60,600, the maximum wage that was covered by Social Security, your government benefit would have replaced about 27% of that amount. If you had earned $85,000, that Social Security benefit would have made up only about 19%. Note that early retirees now collect 80% of the full benefit if they start receiving checks at age 62. That percentage will decline to 75% in 2005 and 70% in 2022 as the age for full benefits rises. Don't count on your pension to pick up what Social Security doesn't cover. What you collect will be based on years of service and your salary over the past three to five years that you were on the job. Pensions typically replace about 30% of pre-retirement salary and rarely increase with inflation.

# How to Size Up a Company Offer

Several years ago, Michael Yendrzeski and 5,800 other Eastman Kodak employees as young as 47 received buy-out offers they felt they couldn't refuse. The package included full pensions, health insurance for life, two weeks' salary for each year of service and bridge payments of as much as $900 a month until they could collect Social Security at 62. Yendrzeski, then 50, walked away from his job as a senior product engineer with $400,000 counting a $900-a-month bridge benefit. With Michael pulling down $900 or so a week as a consultant and his wife Deborah earning $25,000 a year as a dental hygienist, the couple's annual income recently totaled nearly $73,000. And the lump sum from Kodak is quietly growing in a tax-deferred IRA. "We're now living just as well as ever but our total assets have tripled," explains Yendrzeski. "For me, the only question was, why would anyone not do this?"

That same question now haunts the Kodak workers who didn't take the offer. Two years later, Kodak began involuntary layoffs that aim to reduce its work force by 10,000. Those getting the ax received a far less generous good-bye than the 1991 departees. The deal included up to a year of severance but no pension boosts and health insurance for just four months.

There's a costly lesson for employees of Kodak and other big corporations in the enduring era of buyouts. If you're offered a package that looks reasonable, take the money and run because a less generous deal may come your way in a year or two. And it may not be voluntary. How likely are you to face a buyout? If you're over 55 and a manager in a shrinking industry such as manufacturing or retailing, employment experts rate your chances at about one in four.

Companies generally use two types. First are early retirement offers made to workers of 55 and over. If you get one and you're lucky, it will include an enhanced pension such as Yendrzeski's. On the other hand, you might be presented with one that doesn't give you a bridge to Social Security or excludes health insurance. The number of downsizing companies that offer early retirement incentives fluctuates widely from year to year. One reason is that these packages are expensive and must conform to elaborate federal nondiscrimination rules. As a cheaper alternative, employees of all ages are offered arrangements called voluntary separation packages. They typically add up to enough to tide a family over for a year at most.

Accepting either variety of buyout may make sense. First, however, you need to explore these key issues to determine whether the offer works in your favor.

**What choices you may encounter.** Under federal law, you can't be forced to take a package. But the law doesn't prevent an employer from later firing you, eliminating your job, demoting you, cutting your pay or otherwise making you wish that you had taken the buyout. So before turning it down, make sure your company wants you to stay. For example, if your boss seems happy with your performance and the offer is company-wide, you can probably afford to ignore it. If your boss is unhappy, or the offer is targeted at a specific division or department, you ought to give it serious thought. Another tension heightener is that you usually won't have more than two or three months to think things over. If you feel you must take the package but worry that you aren't financially prepared to leave work, you might read the crash-course book *Retirement: Ready or Not* by New York financial planner Lee Rosenberg.

**What to look for in early-out deals.** In an offer extended only to employees older than 50 or 55, an employer will usually adjust your pension to make it bigger than you'd otherwise deserve. We're talking about a traditional defined-benefit pension. Vested money in a profit-sharing or 401(k) savings plan will be yours whenever you leave work. The most common pension adjustment technique is to add several years to your age, length of service or both so as to fatten your payout. Your company may also have elected to provide a financial bridge to Social Security that equals some or all of the payments you will be eligible to receive from the government starting at 62. If you're bridged from age 60, for example, the effect is like starting to get your Social Security checks two years early.

### What to look for in separation deals. Here you get only a cash incentive to leave, usually two or three weeks' salary for each year of your service, up to a maximum of a year's pay. A poor package might include only a week of pay for each year of service, or the offer might top out at 26 weeks and give you no health insurance. A good deal might offer as much as a month of pay per year plus health insurance for a year or more. In addition, if you're vested in your company's pension plan, you'll get it when you reach your employer's regular retirement age.

### What to make of a generous offer. Having to decide whether to volunteer for a package comes down to this question—can you afford to retire? Even if the buyout, plus your other assets, gives you enough to meet your short-term needs, you may not be able to finance all of your retirement years, particularly if your prospects for getting another job are dim. And bear in mind that even the most generous deal won't deliver the same income you would get by staying on until normal retirement. One reason is that your pension rises with your salary. After retirement, however, most pensions don't keep up with inflation. (For details, see "When It Pays to Stay on the Job" on page 52.)

### What about health coverage. While early retirement offers often include lifetime health insurance, voluntary severances typically don't. But you have the right to continue in your firm's medical plan for 18 months at your own expense. After that, you'll have to buy private coverage. This can cost as much as $5,000 a year, if

# When It Pays to Stay on the Job

Even a generous early-out package won't make up for the bigger pension you'd earn by staying on the job. In the table below, we analyze an offer to a 55-year-old who earns $50,000 and has worked 20 years for a company. The package adds five years to both his age and years of service, which gives him the pension he would normally get at 60, and pays him an additional $6,800 for seven years. That's two-thirds of his expected Social Security benefit at 62. The table shows that if he turns down the deal and works until 60 or 62, he will boost his annual retirement income by as much as $8,890. Here are the components of that figure: about $6,890 in additional pension, some $1,600 from his fatter 401(k) plan and $400 from his higher Social Security benefit.

| Age | Income with retirement at 55 without the package | Income with retirement at 55 with the package | Income with retirement at age 60 | Income with retirement at age 62 |
|---|---|---|---|---|
| 55 | $9,073 | $21,177 | $51,500 | $51,500 |
| 56 | 9,073 | 21,177 | 53,000 | 53,000 |
| 57 | 9,073 | 21,177 | 54,600 | 54,600 |
| 58 | 9,073 | 21,177 | 56,300 | 56,300 |
| 59 | 9,073 | 21,177 | 58,000 | 58,000 |
| 60 | 9,073 | 21,177 | 17,354 | 59,700 |
| 61 | 9,073 | 21,177 | 17,354 | 61,500 |
| 62[1] | 19,273 | 24,577 | 27,754 | 33,468 |
| 63 | 19,273 | 24,577 | 27,754 | 33,468 |
| 64 | 19,273 | 24,577 | 27,754 | 33,468 |
| 65 | 19,273 | 24,577 | 27,754 | 33,468 |

**Note:** The table assumes that the employee's pension is based on his five highest years of earnings, that he gets 3% annual pay hikes, and that he contributes 3% of salary to his 401(k), which he annuitizes at retirement. [1]Social Security kicks in. **Source:** Kwasha Lipton

Call It Quits Earlier With Confidence

you're over 50, until Medicare kicks in at 65. If you're not healthy, you may not be able to obtain coverage.

**What about income in retirement.** If you have prospects of another job or plan to start your own business, you may have more latitude to accept an offer that isn't perfect, particularly if you have a working spouse. Consider the example of LaMarr Hamilton, 54, of Vista, Calif. He had worked as an IBM computer technician for 26 years when he took a voluntary severance package. IBM offered him a year's salary of $45,000 plus full health, dental and life insurance. At 55, Hamilton could start collecting a $1,380-a-month pension. If he died before his wife Sally, 52, she would receive $700 a month for life. Bolstered by $350,000 in assets, Sally's $20,000 income as a medical secretary and the guarantee of another job, LaMarr decided to take the offer. Now earning $43,000 as a computer technician for a retailer, he has invested much of his buyout cash in stocks. He expects his investments to grow to $1.5 million by 2002, enabling him to retire early with an income of at least $3,000 a month. That's 80% of his old IBM salary.

 ## Do You Want a Post-Job Job?

Career switching and part-time employment are the rage among retirees who are seeking an escape from the paralyzing boredom that afflicts so many of their peers. What with longer, healthier lives and earlier, richer retirements, Americans face the prospect of decades of active, useful living after they receive the golden handshake. What sensible person whose life has largely been defined by the workplace would want to laze through so many potentially fruitful years? Here are answers to some of the first questions you are apt to ask about that next big step.

**Why work after I retire?** To begin with, you may have no other choice. Inflation, poor planning and an inadequate company pension may force the issue. And even if you don't need a job to make ends meet, you may decide that you want one just to help you keep active and healthy. Those are both benefits that become increasingly more crucial as you get older.

**Does it pay to keep working?** If you're well off, you could wind up losing money by working. Social Security and tax code provisions penalize people who earn too much in retirement. If you're 62 to 64, you couldn't have earned more than roughly $8,160 a year and still received your full Social Security check. The penalty for earning more is a stiff 50¢ deducted from your benefit for each dollar in salary that you made above $8,160. Retirees 65 or older could have earned up to roughly $11,280 and collected full benefits. The penalty for earning more is 33¢ on each additional dollar. (The dollar limits increase annually with inflation.) After 70, there's no benefit loss no matter how much you make. In addition, you are taxed on up to 50% of your Social Security benefits if the total of your adjusted gross income, nontaxable interest, and half of your Social Security benefits exceeds $25,000 ($32,000 if you are married). If that total exceeds $34,000 ($44,000 for couples), you owe tax on up to 85% of your benefits. If you keep working past 65, your benefits will rise by a certain percentage each year until age 70. These increases range from 3% to 8% depending on the year of your birth.

**How should I plan another career?** Start as soon as you can—certainly well before you call it quits. If you want to change fields, you should begin planning at least five years before you retire. This will give you time to take classes and meet people in your field of interest. Even if you want to stay in the same field, it's a good idea to start research on potential employers a year before your planned retirement.

**What's the best way to find a job?** Most career counselors answer this question with the buzz word networking. Make a list of friends, relatives, business relations, old school chums and even distant acquaintances who may be able to help you find a job, whether it is in your old field or a new one. You can often make useful contacts at career seminars or by joining professional organizations. If you don't know anyone at a company that you are interested in, try to find out the name of the person who has the power to hire you. Look in the *Reference Book of Corporate Managements* or in the *Standard & Poor's Register* (both are available at most libraries). Or phone the personnel department at the company. Then write a letter to that executive detailing your skills and interests. After a week or so, follow up with a phone call. Be cordial but persistent. You typically will have to be interviewed by scores of people, and it may take up to a year before a job offer materializes.

**Are pensioners paid less?** The practice of offering lower pay to workers who already are receiving pensions exists at many companies, but habits are changing. Federal law protects older job seekers from arbitrary hiring and salary discrimination. And employers are coming to appreciate that older workers are usually well worth full pay. If you are asked your salary expectations, be assertive. To protect yourself from being shortchanged, find out what the average salary is for the position you want. Career counselors or library research can help. Should you meet the job qualifications for a position in your old field, it's only fair that you should request the middle to high end of the salary range. If you are changing fields and need additional training, you should expect your salary to be at the low end of the scale.

**Should I start a business?** Probably not. While independence sounds exhilarating, don't forget that 66% of small businesses fail within five years, often because of poor planning or lack of funds. Before you embark on what could be a financially and emotionally devastating experience, ask yourself the following questions (more than one or two nays should give you pause). Do I have a product or service that is really needed? Do I have financial backing or money of my own that I can afford to lose? Am I happy working alone? Most telling, do I consider myself a risk taker? Someone who's been a middle manager at the same company for 30 years may not have what it takes to become an entrepreneur. If you are convinced that you are one, you should seek advice from people who have started their own businesses. The Service Corps of Retired Executives, which is sponsored by the Small Business Administration, provides free advice on starting your own business. Look for it in the phone book under U.S. Government/SBA/SCORE.

**What about training and placement?** Your first and best source is your employer. That's because more and more companies offer job planning and counseling. Another option is to phone your state job training or employment service (look in the phone book under State Government Offices). Many have listings for older workers or can at least direct you to placement services in your area. Private career counselors provide occupational testing, one-on-one counseling and training in job-search skills. But if your employer doesn't pay the fees for you, be prepared for charges that can run into the thousands. Another excellent source of help is the growing number of nonprofit organizations that are set up to assist older workers. You can write for information about nonpaying consulting work to the National Executive Service Corps (257 Park Avenue South, New York, N.Y. 10010), a volunteer placement service for retired executives. Small and medium-size firms recruit via its Senior Career Planning & Placement Service.

**Can I try out a career?** If you don't need to work for money, you should explore the field of volunteering. Often this can later turn into a paid job. There's a big advantage to starting this way. You can set your own schedule and contribute your time to a cause that may give you great satisfaction. Volunteer opportunities abound in hospitals, day care centers, libraries, schools and many other community or charitable organizations.

# 4

# Blunt the Tax Man's Big Bite

There's no reason for Americans to wait patiently for the party leaders in Congress to get their tax-trimming and budget-reduction acts together. In this chapter, we offer retirement-related ways to cut your income taxes this year and beyond plus advice on likely changes in the law. We also show you which states currently levy the least and how best to minimize the tax bills on your investment portfolio and future retirement check. As the tax landscape shifts over the next few years, sound planning will become even more important. Begin with the tips below that apply directly to retirement.

**Start funding an IRA.** Individual Retirement Accounts offer tremendous advantages to younger savers. You get to deduct a full $2,000 annual contribution as long as your adjusted gross income is $25,000 or less if you're single, $40,000 or less if you are married and file jointly. (AGI is your total income minus a few tax-favored items, such as alimony you pay. Taxable income, the amount on which your tax rate is based, is your AGI minus your deductions and exemptions.) If your spouse works, you can each contribute $2,000 to your respective IRAs. What's more, odds are strong that Congress will pass a "back-end" IRA in the future. This would permit nondeductible annual contributions of up to $4,000 per couple ($2,000 for singles). Like a traditional IRA, the earnings would grow tax deferred. Then after five years you could make withdrawals tax-free if you used the money for retirement, a first-home purchase, college or large medical expenses. One Republican proposal would even let you convert all or part of your current IRA to a back-end account, not including rollovers from employer-sponsored plans. To do so, you would have to pay income tax on the previously untaxed portion of the IRA, although you could spread the tax over four years. For now, however, you're better off with a deductible IRA. Later you can convert to a back-end account if you need the money.

**Exploit your state's breaks.** The IRS estimates that nearly 8 million Americans overpaid their state and local tax bills because they didn't realize they were eligible for special breaks. To learn about such goodies, curl up with the instruction booklet for your state tax return. You'll be the richer for spending time with it. For example, if you're retired and collecting Social Security benefits, they won't be taxed in Alabama, Arizona, Arkansas, California, Delaware, Georgia, Hawaii, Idaho, Illinois, Indiana, Kentucky, Louisiana, Maine, Maryland, Massachusetts, Michigan, Mississippi, New Jersey, New York, North Carolina, Ohio, Oklahoma, Oregon, Pennsylvania, South Carolina, Virginia and the District of Columbia. And at least a portion of a retiree's pension is exempt from taxes in Alabama, Arkansas, Colorado, Delaware, Georgia, Hawaii, Illinois, Louisiana, Maryland, Michigan, Mississippi, Montana, New Jersey, New Mexico, New York, North Carolina, Oregon, Pennsylvania, South Carolina and Utah.

**Defend your lower-tax abode.** Watch out if you own dwellings in two states and work part of the time in the state with the higher taxes. In recent years, California, New York and other high-tax states have begun taxing the entire income of such residents including interest, dividends and capital gains earned in other states. What to do? First, find out what constitutes taxable residency in each state where you work or own property. Most states won't consider you a resident unless you spend more than half the year at a home within their borders. But New York and other voracious

# Avoid Those Onerous IRA Penalties

The IRS penalizes over a million people annually for taking money out of their IRAs too early—or too late. Folks who withdrew money before age 59.5 had to pay a 10% penalty on top of ordinary income taxes. Those who didn't start taking out money by 70.5 paid 50% of the amount that they should have withdrawn. Both of these stiff tax blows, however, can be avoided by heeding the following advice.

✦ **Early withdrawals.** To tap your IRA without penalty before 59.5, you must make annual withdrawals that could conceivably last for the rest of your life. To calculate the appropriate amounts, first obtain an IRS life expectancy table (call 800-829-3676 and request Form 590). Then divide the value of your IRA by the number of years the table indicates you may live. For example, a 52-year-old with a $500,000 IRA can anticipate sticking around another 31 years. So he or she would have to withdraw approximately $16,000 a year. You must continue to take this amount annually for five years or until you turn 59.5, whichever is later. Before starting withdrawals, be sure you require that much money. If you need, say, $10,000 this year, that's an extra $40,000 you must take out of the account in the subsequent years. Thus a big chunk of your savings won't grow tax-deferred.

✦ **Late withdrawals.** You can defer these until age 70.5. After that you must take out an IRS-approved minimum amount each year. To calculate it, you have to divide your IRA balance by your life expectancy. If you don't want to take that much, write to the financial services company holding your IRA and designate a beneficiary. You may then calculate the minimum withdrawal using your joint life expectancies listed in the IRS table. For example, a 71-year-old woman has a single life expectancy of around 15 years. If she has accumulated a $500,000 IRA, she must take out at least $32,680 a year. But if she includes her 61-year-old husband in the calculation, their joint life expectancy of 25 years would reduce the minimum to $19,763.

✦ **What if you die first?** Then your spouse or other beneficiary can roll over the IRA into his or her own account, name a child or grandchild as a new beneficiary and recalculate the minimum withdrawal. The IRS insists that the child's age, for purposes of the calculation, be figured as no more than 10 years less than your beneficiary's age. So if your spouse is 70 and the grandchild is 15, the minimum must be computed as if the child were 60. When the child inherits the IRA, the minimum could be recalculated again, using his or her actual life expectancy.

states may try to tax your entire income if you spend as little as one month within their borders. How can you document that your home in the low-tax state is your main residence? Keep records that show where you spend most of your time, such as phone and electricity bills. Also keep documents showing where you go to church, register your car and vote.

**Set up a defined-benefit Keogh.** If you're 45 or older and generate income from self-employment, investigate this potential monster of a tax shelter. Like other defined-benefit pensions, this special type of Keogh is based on your life expectancy plus the amount you want to draw down as an annuity when you retire. The maximum benefit you can receive is your average income over your three top earning years or $120,000, whichever is less. Hiring an actuary to administer such a plan isn't cheap (up to $3,000 to set one up plus around $1,250 a year). You have until year-end to open a Keogh, though you can fund the plan through the April 15 filing deadline.

**Seek out a rabbi trust.** Many companies now offer their highly paid executives so-called rabbi trusts (because the method was first used by a congregation for its rabbi). Your employer sets up an irrevocable trust, stashes money in it every year for you and pays the income tax on the fund. You then have retirement dollars building up to be spent when you are presumably in a lower tax bracket. One drawback is that you have no control over your trust, which can even be seized by creditors to pay your employer's debts. So be confident about your company's long-term health before asking for the rabbi's blessing.

 ## Defend Your Retirement Check

It's a frightening thought. You're ready to grab the retirement money you built up over your 25-year career, and you suddenly realize that this could be the largest single amount you'll ever see. When a lump-sum pension, 401(k) and other corporate savings plans are totted up, workers can walk away with $1 million or more. Thus your first task is to keep as much of it as possible from the IRS. But beware that your distribution has a short fuse. If you fritter away more than 60 days after receiving the money before deciding what to do with it, the amount may be subject to a 10% penalty as well as federal tax.

You have two ways to ease the blow. You can take the money and use a tax-cutting technique called special averaging. Or you can roll over your payout into an IRA and postpone paying the tax until you withdraw the money, presumably when you'll be in a lower tax bracket than you are now. Which method is better depends mostly on the size of your settlement and how long you have until you stop working altogether. Before making a choice, you need to understand the main points of both approaches.

**Average over five or 10 years.** You may qualify for either five- or 10-year averaging, depending on your age. Both can yield after-tax results that are far more favorable than paying up in a single year. As the name suggests, this legerdemain computes your tax as if you received the distribution over a five- or 10-year period. There are entry rules, however. To use averaging, your lump-sum distribution must meet the following four requirements. It must be:

♦   A qualified pension, profit-sharing or Keogh plan in which you participated at least five years. Your plan administrator can tell you whether the plan qualifies.

♦   The entire balance that is due to you from all of your employer's qualified retirement plans.

♦   Paid to you within a single tax year. If you retire this year and pay taxes on a calendar-year basis, you must receive your entire balance by December 31.

♦ Paid after you turn 59.5. The age test doesn't apply, however, if you were born before January 1, 1936.

## How to figure the tax.

If you meet all those tests, you can apply averaging to the taxable portion of your lump-sum distribution. This includes your employer's contributions to your account and its earnings over the years—but not your own nondeductible contributions. The taxable amount is listed on the Form 1099-R that you will receive from your employer. If your distribution is less than $70,000, part of it is absolutely tax-free thanks to the minimum-distribution allowance. This break exempts 50% of the first $20,000 of a lump-sum distribution from tax. As the payout rises above $20,000, however, the tax-free portion phases out. At $30,000, $8,000 is tax-free. At $40,000, it's $6,000. At $50,000, it's $4,000. At $60,000, it's $2,000. And at $70,000 or more, it's zero.

The tax on the rest of the distribution is figured using grade school math. First, you divide the remaining distribution by five. Next, find the tax on the result using the rates for single taxpayers; the rates are listed in the IRS instruction booklet for filing your annual tax return. Finally, multiply that tax by five. Say you receive a lump-sum distribution of $180,000 that includes no nondeductible contributions by you. The payout is too big to benefit from the minimum-distribution allowance, so the entire amount will be taxable. Using five-year averaging, one-fifth of $180,000 is $36,000. Tax on that amount is about $7,214. Multiplying $7,214 by five gives you a tax bill of $36,070. Without using averaging, the tax could run as high as $71,280 (39.6% of $180,000).

If you were born before 1936, you may use 10-year averaging, which works the same way as its five-year cousin except that you divide and multiply by 10 instead of five. There's one catch, however: With 10-year averaging, you must use the higher and more steeply graduated 1986 tax rates for singles, which ranged from 11% to 50%.

If you qualify to average over five or 10 years, use Form 4972 to figure your tax both ways and choose the one that results in the lower bill. You might also compare it with what your tax would be if you didn't use averaging. If the difference is small and you don't plan to quit working altogether, you might want to pay the regular tax. The reason is that you can use averaging only once. If you expect a bigger lump-sum distribution from another qualified plan in the future, you might postpone taking advantage of averaging until you retire for good. Your tax can be even lower if you were born before January 1, 1936 and earned retirement benefits before 1974. In that case, you may treat part of the payout as a capital gain and pay a flat 20% tax on it. That can be a bargain compared with current income tax rates of up to 39.6% and the top capital-gains rate of 28%. Your employer will tell you how much qualifies.

**The case for tax-free rollovers.** To postpone taxes on your lump sum, you can roll it over into an IRA and let the money grow tax deferred until you withdraw it. If you wish, you can stash the distribution in two or more IRAs, for example, putting part in a stock fund and the rest in a bond fund. If you have a Keogh retirement plan set up with self-employment earnings, you can fend off the IRS with a rollover and keep your averaging over five or 10 years. Invest your company-plan distribution in the Keogh. Then, if you later take a lump-sum distribution from it, you can use averaging to figure the tax.

The basic rollover rules are simple. It must be completed within 60 days of receiving the distribution. The money can then be placed in a new or existing IRA. If your lump sum is paid in installments over the calendar year, the 60-day rule applies to each of the payments. If you are unlucky enough to miss the deadline, you'll owe tax on all the money plus a 10% penalty if you're under age 59.5. Once made, the rollover can't be revoked. Ask your employer to transfer the money directly to the IRA of your choice. If you make the rollover yourself, 20% of the payout will be withheld under IRS rules, and you will have to claim a credit on your next tax return to get it back. Worse, if you're under 59.5, you'll have to pay the nonrefundable 10% early-withdrawal penalty on the 20% unless you make it up out of your own pocket. Don't include your after-tax contributions to the plan or lump-sum severance pay in the rollover. If you do, the IRS will levy a 6% excise tax on the excess amount.

Keep in mind that you don't have to roll over your entire distribution. You can take some of the money and pay tax on it plus a 10% penalty if you're under age 59.5. (In this case, however, you can't use averaging.) The amount rolled over will still escape taxes until withdrawn from your IRA. You must report a rollover on line 16 of your 1040 but only for information purposes. If not, the IRS will assume you're omitting income and send you a bill for additional tax.

**Which method is better?** Don't rush into either one blindly. Remember too that a rollover merely postpones the tax man's inevitable payday. In fact, if you are in a higher tax bracket when you withdraw the money, a rollover could actually wind up costing you more than simply paying your tax when you take your distribution. Before electing a rollover, have your tax pro or financial planner compute the current tax on your lump-sum distribution using one or more of the methods described earlier. Compare this amount to an estimate of the tax you'll pay on future distributions from an IRA. Make sure your pro takes into account the money you'll earn in the IRA.

Chances are the rollover will win hands down. Consider a new retiree who at 62 receives $250,000 from his company's 401(k) at the start of this year. He plans to let the money grow at 6.5% annually in an IRA until 72 and then withdraw the money gradually over the next 15 years. He expects to be in the combined 34% federal and state bracket during those years. Thus his best bet is clearly a rollover. The $250,000, undiminished by taxes, will grow to $440,643 by the time he turns 72. In sharp contrast, with 10-year averaging, his after-tax $205,882 (his $250,000 payout minus an immediate tax of $44,118) will increase to just $300,471 at age 72. By choosing a rollover, you'll avoid the 15% tax penalty on what the government deems to be excess annual distributions from a retirement plan—$148,500 at last count. (The amount rises each year with inflation.) You alternatively can take an amount that doesn't exceed the excise tax limit and shield the rest in an IRA. Of course, you may need all the money immediately. In that case, you should pay the tax using averaging and be assured that you've done all you can to shield your precious lump from tax meltdown.

 ## Keep More of Your Portfolio's Profit

The best news for many aspiring retirees is the good possibility of a tax cut on capital gains. That's the profit you clear when you sell an investment that has risen in value as opposed to the dividends or interest you collect along the way. Better yet, the favorable tax treatment accorded such gains, which heretofore has solely benefited people with high incomes, may soon be available to all taxpayers, regardless of income.

Under federal tax law, you pay no more than 28% on gains from investments held for at least a year. That's a good deal less than the tax on your income if you are in the 31%, 36% or 39.6% brackets. (If you're in the 15% or 28% bracket, your gains tax is the same as your regular marginal tax rate.) But many of the Republican leaders in Congress want to cut the tax on long-term capital gains to half of an investor's top income tax rate. That means people in the 39.6% bracket (at last count, taxable earnings above $256,500) would cede only about 19.8% of their gains to Uncle Sam. Those in the lowest 15% bracket, including many teenagers and retirees, would pay a super-low 7.5%.

Here are the tax basics of various investments. In each case, we point to the most tax-efficient choices and show the steps you can take now to lighten the tax burden on your profits. The advice is important because

# How to Figure All Your Capital Gains

To compute a gain or loss when you sell a stock or mutual fund, take the proceeds of the sale and subtract your basis—or cost of acquiring the shares. Sounds simple. But the tax code can make it tricky depending on how you obtained the stock. Follow these general rules.

| IF YOU GOT STOCK BY... | ...YOUR BASIS IS |
|---|---|
| Buying it directly | The price you paid for the shares plus any fees or commissions you paid to buy them. Fees or commissions on the sale do not add to your basis but can be subtracted from the proceeds, thus also reducing your gain. |
| A dividend reinvestment plan (DRIP) | The full market value of the stock on the date the dividend was paid plus any fees or commissions even if, as is often the case, the DRIP lets you buy shares at a discount. |
| Receiving it as a gift | The donor's original basis plus any gift tax the donor has to pay. Exception: if you later sell the stock for a loss, your basis is the lesser of the donor's basis or the stock's fair market value on the date the gift was given. |
| Inheriting it | The market value of the shares on the date you inherited them. This often is the same as the donor's date of death. But in some cases the executor may choose an "alternate valuation date." To check, ask the executor or review the estate tax return. Note that even if you sell the stock within a year, any profit is considered a long-term rather than a short-term capital gain because the stock was inherited. |
| Receiving it after a stock split | The same, for your total stake, as it was before the split. To find out your new per-share basis, take the original basis of your holding and divide it by the number of shares you own after the split became effective. |
| Obtaining it as a stock dividend | Whatever the company tells you it is. How's that? Sometimes a company issues a dividend in the form of stock or spins off part of its business and gives shareholders stock in the new firm. You usually won't owe any tax on this so-called stock distribution even if it came as a dividend. But the per-share basis of your holding will be reduced by a percentage that the company will calculate and report to you. |
| Exercising a stock option | The price you paid for the shares (plus fees or commissions) even though it is lower than the market value at the time of purchase. You must retain the shares for at least a year after buying them, and for two years after receiving the option, or else any profit from their sale will be taxed as ordinary income rather than capital gains. |

taxes take a bigger toll on investments than most people realize. Taxation at today's rates would have zapped from 7% to 37% of the total return of assorted stock, bond and real estate holdings over the past 10 years. "Income taxes are at their highest since 1982," observes John Bogle, chairman of the Vanguard family of mutual funds. "So the risks investors face are the same as ever, but their potential returns are lower."

The tax code is filled with quirks that let you defer, reduce or even avoid taxes. To postpone the tax bite, you can concentrate on growth investments, where the profit comes mostly from price appreciation (taxable when you sell) rather than current income (taxed in the year you collect it). You can further reduce taxes by timing your sales, especially of losers. And you can avoid taxes altogether by choosing the right kinds of bonds or, if you own real estate, by swapping your old property for new property to duck the tax that would ordinarily be due. The message here is to be smart about taxes, not fanatical. While it is important to reduce investment taxes, that should not be your only goal. Go for the most promising investment. Use what you learn here to make sure that it will still be the most rewarding choice after you pay the taxes.

 ## How to Shield Your Stocks

It's not what you earn as an investor that counts; it's what you keep after the taxman takes his cut. Growth stocks, which deliver most of their return through price gains, enjoy a major tax advantage over income stocks, which pay high dividends. Not only are price gains subject to a maximum levy of 28%, vs. 39.6% for dividends, but the tax isn't due until you cash out, leaving more of your money invested. Here are MONEY's tax-savvy tips for investing in stock. The first three apply only to people in at least the 31% bracket (which lately started at $56,551 for singles and $94,251 for couples), though they eventually may work for everyone if Congress ever cuts back the tax on long-term capital gains sufficiently. The remaining points generally apply to all investors.

## Go for growth in taxable portfolios. Keeping a growth stock in an IRA or Keogh is like buying a Ferrari to drive to your commuter bus stop. You don't really need the account's tax protection because growth stocks derive 90% of their return from price increase, which isn't taxed until you sell. You also forgo the right to use any losses you incur to offset gains or ordinary income. When you finally withdraw your earnings from the account, you'll pay tax at the rates for ordinary income (which run as high as 39.6%) rather than at the maximum 28% capital-gains rate.

## Seek income in tax-deferred accounts. Your IRA, Keogh and the like provide a comfy home for high-dividend stocks whose payouts would be taxed each year. Good candidates include utility stocks (they generally pay 6% to 7% a year in dividends), financial services firms (2% to 4%) and many blue chips.

## Shoot for long-term price gains. The favorable tax treatment of capital gains applies only to assets held at least a year. If you cash out sooner,  you'll pay your marginal income tax rate. So unless you've got hold of a real rocket—say, a stock that doubled in eight months but now seems headed for a fall—stay invested for at least 12 months before ejecting.

## Sell your priciest shares first. Let's suppose that you have bought a company's shares at various prices over the years and now want to unload some for a profit. Since the tax code lets you designate which shares you sell, dump the ones that cost you the most in order to hold down your capital gains. Sure, you'll pay tax on those gains someday. In general, however, it's better to pay tax in the future rather than today.

## Donate stocks to good causes. The next time you want to be generous to a tax-exempt group, give away

# When Should You Take Social Security?

That's the No. 1 question for many retirees. Fully 62% of men and 73% of women begin at 62 even though they get only 80% of the benefits they would be due if they waited until 65. Whether you should follow the crowd depends on your financial circumstances, your plans for working in retirement and your willingness to gamble on your longevity. At 62, a man can expect to live for another 18 years, a woman for 22 years. Here is the basic explanation of your options.

✦ **Start early.** The rule of thumb is that you should consider collecting your first check at 62 if Social Security benefits will amount to less than 50% of your retirement income, or if your net worth, excluding your home, is more than $100,000. That way, you can enjoy the extra income in your early retirement years and still have plenty of assets for your later years. Here's why. Let's assume you're eligible for an annual Social Security benefit of $12,000 at 65. If you file for it at 62, you'll get only $9,600 a year. Even so, by 65, you will have pocketed a total of $28,800. You won't reach the break-even point until 74 (when the total of all your Social Security checks will be the same as if you had waited to file for benefits at 65). If you can afford to invest your Social Security checks, you can extend the break-even point even farther.

✦ **Wait until 65 or even later.** You probably should postpone collecting benefits until you can get bigger checks at 65 if Social Security will provide 50% or more of your retirement income, or if your net worth, excluding your home, is less than $100,000. The life expectancy of a male or female is greater than the break-even point. So if you base your decision on the odds, you're better off waiting until 65. If you put off collecting benefits beyond 65, you will be rewarded with even bigger checks. But the actuarial odds generally favor people who begin cashing in at 65. Postponing benefits is the only sensible decision when you hold a job in retirement that pays more than $8,160 a year (if you're between 62 and 65) or $11,280 (between 65 and 70). The amount rises yearly with inflation. When earnings top these limits, the government will cut your benefits $1 for every $2 of excess pay from age 62 to 65 and $1 for every $3 between the ages of 65 and 70. Once you turn 70, however, you'll receive a full benefit regardless of how much you earn from your hard labor. Of course, keep in mind that you'll have to continue paying FICA tax on your earnings even while Social Security is paying you.

appreciated stock instead of cash. Why? Imagine that you bought a stock for $5,000 a decade ago and that it's now worth $15,000. If you cash out, you'll owe tax of up to 28% (or $2,800) on that $10,000 gain. But if you give the stock to charity, the organization pockets the full $15,000 value because it doesn't have to pay tax on capital gains. And you get to take the same $15,000 tax deduction that you would have taken if you'd donated cash instead of stock even though your shares are worth only $12,200 to you after taxes.

**Time losses to claim a tax prize.** Every investor winds up holding losing cards. But at least you can deduct the damage outside of a tax-sheltered account. You are allowed to write off capital losses against the full amount of any gains you may reap during the year, and then against as much as $3,000 more of ordinary income. And don't worry if you can't write off the entire loss in one year. You can carry leftover losses forward to future years until they are all used up.

**Avoid these tax tangles.** Watch out for the wash sale rule that prohibits you from deducting a loss on the sale of a stock if you buy any shares of the same company within 30 days either before or after that sale. Take into account the commission you paid when you bought a stock, as well as that imposed when you sold it, when figuring your gain or loss. And be sure to claim a U.S. tax credit if foreign tax was withheld from dividends paid to you by an international stock.

 **How to Tame Fund Taxes**

Many mutual fund investors are jolted when they discover they owe tax on a fund that lost money in a given year. Sound impossible? Not at all. It happens because a fund must distribute to shareholders nearly all the yearly income it earned from dividends and interest, plus any net gains it realized from selling securities, even if it had a losing year overall. Don't get irate, get informed. And start by employing the following mutual fund tax tips.

**Favor low turnover and tax savvy.** Funds that follow a buy-and-hold strategy tend to realize fewer capital gains than those that trade actively. So if you are choosing between two funds with otherwise similar performance, go for the one with the lower turnover ratio (the proportion of its assets that have been bought or sold within the past year). You can find the ratio by calling a fund or by looking in its semiannual report. Low turnover is not the only positive indicator. A tax-savvy manager can be an active trader and still hold the tax bite down by timing any losses to offset the fund's gains. When considering a hot fund that has a high turnover ratio, check out its tax-efficiency ratio. That's the percentage of its total return that is left after taxes are paid. After-tax fund winners tend to have tax-efficiency ratios of around 80% or better.

**Go for funds that protect profits.** Several fund companies have launched carefully managed index funds that aim to deliver maximum tax efficiency by timing their losses to offset most of their gains. (Index funds are those that try to match or beat the performance of market benchmarks like the S&P 500 stock index.) Discount broker Charles Schwab has several, including International Index, Schwab 1000 and Small-Cap Index. The Vanguard fund family entries include Capital Appreciation Portfolio, Growth & Income Portfolio and Balanced Portfolio.

**Invest overseas in taxable accounts.** Under tax treaties between the U.S. and foreign countries, funds that are more than half invested outside the U.S. typically have to pay 5% to 10% of whatever they earn on those holdings to the foreign governments (just as you would if you owned a foreign stock). In return, you are eligible for as much as a dollar-for-dollar reduction of your U.S. tax provided you hold the funds in a taxable account. If you park them in a tax-deferred retirement account, however, the credit is worthless.

# How to Shelter Real Estate Income

You can deduct the interest you pay on mortgages totaling as much as $1 million on your first and second homes even if you rent out that second home part of the year. If you buy real estate strictly as an investment, you can depreciate (write off) the full price over the next 27.5 or 39 years. And if you help manage the property by, say, setting rents, you can deduct any operating losses against as much as $25,000 of non-investment income. With stocks and bonds, this kind of deduction is limited to $3,000 a year. Even REITs (real estate investment trusts), which own interests in property or mortgages and trade like stocks, have certain tax advantages. If your REIT profits from the sale of a property, you pay tax on your share at the maximum long-term gains rate of 28%, not at the generally higher rate for short-term gains. That's true even if the REIT owned the asset for less than a year.

If you want to unload a highly appreciated piece of property but stay invested in real estate, you can duck capital-gains tax with a nifty maneuver that's called a "like kind exchange." Here's how one works. You, as exchanger, transfer the deed to your property to a buyer. The buyer gives his payment to an intermediary, often an attorney. You then have 45 days to identify property you want to buy and 180 days to close on it. At the closing on the second property, the intermediary pays the seller (you chip in too if the new property is worth more than the old) and the seller gives you his deed. You now own the property you want—and owe no tax on the real estate you traded away.

# Don't Own a Policy on Your Life

Who owns your life insurance policy? If you're like most people, the answer is you. And it may be a costly error. Why? If you own the policy, the proceeds that are paid out when you die could get whacked by estate taxes of

37% to 55%. Here are the possible tax consequences of four common ways to own life insurance policies.

♦ **Insured as owner.** At your death, the IRS will count the insurance proceeds as part of your estate. If the death benefit pushes the estate's value above $600,000, the excess is subject to federal estate tax.

♦ **Spouse as owner.** If he or she owns the policy, the proceeds won't be taxed. If your spouse names someone else as beneficiary, such as a child, the IRS considers the death benefit to be a gift. Any amount that's above $10,000 may be subject to 37% to 55% tax.

♦ **Nonspousal beneficiary as owner.** The IRS won't consider the policy part of your taxable estate, and the beneficiary won't owe tax on the proceeds. But if you give a policy to the beneficiary, the IRS sees the transfer as a gift. That's not a problem with term insurance; the policy has no value until you die. With a cash-value policy, you may trigger gift taxes if the cash value exceeds $10,000. If you die within three years of giving away any type of life policy, the death benefit will still be included in your taxable estate. After you've transferred your policy to the beneficiary, you may pay the premium with no tax consequences, as long as it doesn't exceed $10,000 a year.

♦ **Trust as owner.** The IRS won't count the death benefit as part of your taxable estate, and the trust's beneficiaries will get the proceeds tax-free. With a trust, you're subject to the same gift-tax limitations that apply if the beneficiary owns the policy. So why have a trust own the policy? Because you gain more flexibility with a trust, which can provide steady income to a beneficiary. A trust also can pay the taxes on your estate without the insurance proceeds being included among its assets. For a trust's assets to escape being included in your taxable estate, the trust must be irrevocable. That means you can't change the terms of the trust or terminate it even if your beneficiary is your spouse and you later divorce.

# 5

# Protect Your Nest Egg From Perils

M any people approaching retirement harbor fears of financial disaster. But you can side-step potential pitfalls by taking a good hard look at where your net worth is most vulnerable to unexpected assaults—and why. Don't limit your soul searching to the investments and real estate that were covered earlier in this book. Your pension, if you have one, is among your most valuable retirement assets, followed by tax-deferred company savings plans, like 401(k)s, and life insurance policies with sizable cash values. Insuring against threats to your family's health and pre-retirement earning power is also critical. Whether you will wind up living the retirement of your dreams or of your nightmares may depend on how quickly you recognize and overcome the hazards discussed in this chapter. Among them:

**You may not get a pension.** For those lucky enough to have one, the monthly pension check can replace as much as a third of pre-retirement income. These days nearly a third of retirees collect private pensions, compared with only 9% in 1962. But if current trends continue, the heyday of the traditional pension is probably past. Many companies, particularly small ones, are shunning defined-benefit pensions in favor of less expensive defined-contribution plans such as 401(k)s. According to one analysis, the number of defined-benefit plans has dropped 33% in recent years. Starting next year, defined-contribution programs are expected to account for 43% of retirement assets, up from 30% a decade earlier. With a defined benefit, employees are guaranteed a fixed monthly payout for life and usually are not required to make contributions of their own. By contrast, defined contributions are funded primarily by employees, who also make investment decisions and assume all risk. Thus the plan may never amount to much if you fail to contribute enough to it or if you mismanage your investments. In short, you become even more vulnerable to other threats described below.

**Medical benefits could be cut.** Bills for doctors, drugs and hospitals can wreck even the best retirement plans. Employer-sponsored medical coverage is especially crucial for early retirees who are too young to qualify for Medicare, the government insurance program for those age 65 and older. But company coverage is also valuable because it covers most of the costs that Medicare doesn't. Today only a third of all retirees get free or low-cost health insurance from their former employers—and that figure is declining fast. Employers are scaling back partly because they must report the cost of future retiree health benefits on their balance sheets, thereby reducing profits. According to a survey of 2,400 firms, 7% have ended or plan to end benefits for future retirees, 30% have raised premiums for current retirees and 26% have hiked deductibles or co-payments for current retirees. Some who've suffered cutbacks have sued former employers to reinstate promised benefits. But courts so far have ruled that employers have the right to change or terminate such plans as long as documents describing employee and retiree benefits make that position clear.

**Social Security shrinks more.** This squeeze is underway. You now are taxed on up to 50% of your Social Security benefits if the total of your adjusted gross income, nontaxable interest, and half of your Social Security benefits exceeds $25,000 ($32,000 if you are married). If that total exceeds $34,000 ($44,000 for couples), you owe tax on up to 85% of your benefits. If you keep working past 65, your benefits will rise by a certain yearly percentage until age 70. These increases range from 3% to 8% depending on the year of your birth. The age at which you can collect full Social Security benefits, now 65, is scheduled to rise to 66 in 2005 and to 67 in 2022. And experts believe Congress will keep nibbling away at Social Security. The retirement age might be further advanced, all benefits may be taxed and cost-of-living adjustments may even be scaled back or frozen for a while.

**You'll sabotage yourself.** Like most Americans, you represent the single most potent threat to your prosperous retirement. The danger is that you won't put enough aside or that you will squander your savings. The U.S. personal savings rate has stood at around 4% since the late 1980s, half what it was in the 1970s and a scandal compared with other nations. The Japanese save at three times our rate, the Germans double. And despite an increased tendency to retire solo, many singles spend like they expect to retire on someone else's savings. On average, married couples put away 5% of their pretax pay, single men save 3% and single women save less than 2%. More unsettling, most people tend to blow their retirement savings while they are employed. One study found that just 11% of workers who received lump-sum distributions from a tax-deferred retirement account opted to roll over the entire amount into a similar account, while 34% spent all of the payout.

 ## Take the Pulse of Your Pension

Each year about a hundred companies default on their pension plans, stranding both their retirees and workers who are anticipating regular pension checks at retirement. The victims typically turn to the federal PBGC (Pension Benefit Guaranty Corporation), which recently paid $721 million in annual benefits to 174,200 retirees covered by nearly 2,000 plans. The PBGC, a 20-year-old government insurance agency, gets its money both from

Protect Your Nest Egg From Perils

the terminated plans' assets and from premiums paid by most companies that provide employees with traditional defined-benefit pensions.

For many retired managers, however, the PBGC replaces only part of the pension once promised by their employers. With payouts capped by law, the agency lately paid a maximum benefit of around $2,575 a month. Worse, if you took early retirement at age 55, your PBGC benefit plummets to about $1,160 even if you were due more under your former employer's pension rules. If you retired at age 62, benefits max out at $2,033. How likely is your pension to default? The agency estimates that 16,000 of the 64,000 plans it insures are underfunded. Even if your company's program isn't one of the weaklings, it may not be flush enough to keep paying benefits throughout your retirement. So, whether you're retired or still working, it's crucial to determine the odds of your pension lasting the rest of your life. If your pension looks shaky, you can at least get an early start on boosting your savings to ensure that your retirement is comfortable. Here's how to take the pulse of your pension's health.

**Identify your plan's type.** If you're in a defined-contribution program, such as a 401(k), you can relax as long as you're putting as much money in it as you can afford. Your benefit at retirement will depend on how much you've contributed, the amount your employer may have matched and how investments in the plan have fared over the course of time. All this is easy to track because most employers provide quarterly statements of your account's value. Since the account is your property, your company can't legally raid it to pay off its debts. Even if the firm fails, you can transfer your retirement money elsewhere or leave it with the management company that acts as your plan's trustee. That's not the case with a traditional defined-benefit pension. Many companies in shaky financial condition underfund these plans, diverting money to business expenses. That puts your retirement benefits at risk.

## Be Wary of This Private Pension Spiel

Life insurance agents have come up with another novel pitch to peddle policies—use the tax-shelter benefits of your coverage to build your own private pension plan. If you salt away, say, $1,000 a month or more for 20 years into a universal or variable life policy, the salesman explains, the investment portion of the policy (called the cash value) would grow by as much as 12% a year. Then, when you need income for retirement, you could stop paying premiums, withdraw what you've paid in and begin borrowing against the policy through the insurer's free or low-cost loans, which don't have to be repaid. The outstanding loan balance and any interest would be deducted from the death benefit when you die. And the loan proceeds escape income taxes.

Sounds good. But these spiels can be dangerously misleading. The policy's return would shrink if interest rates drop or, in the case of variable life, if the stock market falls. Then your pile for retirement might never materialize. The tax-free loans could also backfire. That's because borrowing could so erode the cash value that you would have to pay more premiums just to keep the policy in force. If the policy lapses, all loans in excess of the premiums you've paid plus any remaining cash value would become taxable. So if you plowed in $12,000 a year for 20 years, then borrowed $40,000 annually for 20 years, and the policy lapsed, you would owe taxes on at least $560,000. That's a $156,800 bill for someone in the 28% federal tax bracket. Our advice? Resist the temptation of these private pensions and stash your savings in 401(k)s and IRAs.

**Check its financial health.** Within 90 days of becoming eligible for the plan, you automatically should receive a booklet summarizing how it operates. For specific information, however, you must ask your employee benefits office for a copy of Form 5500, which the company files each year with the U.S. Department of Labor. If you prefer, you can request the document from the department. Just send your employer's identification number (on last year's W-2 tax form) and the plan number (in the summary booklet) to the Division of Technical Assistance and Inquiries, Pension and Welfare Benefits Administration,

Protect Your Nest Egg From Perils

U.S. Department of Labor, 200 Constitution Ave. N.W., Washington, D.C. 20210. When you receive the Form 5500, pay attention to the actuary's report in the back. If the actuary expresses reservations about the plan's financial health, you have good reason to worry. Of course, even if your plan is sound today, you can't be sure it will be healthy in the future. So obtain Form 5500 every few years to check the actuary's report.

**Look for PBGC life support.** The agency stands behind nearly all private defined-benefit plans. The exceptions are those provided by professional service employers, such as lawyers or doctors, with fewer than 26 employees; church groups with any number of employees; and state, local and federal governments. In addition to the benefit limits described earlier, the PBGC operates under another noteworthy limitation. It steps in only in the event of total default. If your pension plan can scrape together part of your promised benefit, the PBGC won't pony up the difference. If your company can afford to pay more than the PBGC maximum but less than it had promised to pay you, the PBGC will take over the pension and pay you the maximum amount the plan can afford.

Most companies fund their pension obligations appropriately, of course. If they don't and the companies fail to correct shortfalls after repeated warnings, they risk legal action by the Department of Labor and tax penalties from the IRS that could equal as much as the amount of underfunding. Congress tightened the pressure on underfunded pensions in 1994 in part by raising insurance premiums for underfunded plans and requiring any plan less than 90% funded to alert all its beneficiaries. Even so, the PBGC figures about a quarter of companies have not yet funded their plans properly. What can you do in the event that your employer is one of them? Start by dealing with the problem the same way you would any financial setback. Try to economize so that you can get by if you're already retired or save more if you're still working. If you're employed, you should invest as much money as you can in tax-deferred retirement plans such as 401(k)s. In short, if Washington can't reform your employer, you probably can't either. So you'll have to take charge of your own retirement.

## How Divorce Can Crimp Your Plans

Even longstanding marriages can be torn apart when children move out, careers plateau, aged parents die or future options seem to dwindle. The number of divorces among people over age 55 is a third higher than 20 years ago. If your marriage breaks up, your shattered emotions may eventually heal. But your retirement plans might not after you and your ex split your assets. Just how a divorcing couple's assets are divided up can depend on the state they live in. While all courts must follow federal law in dealing with company-sponsored retirement plans, states have their own laws on splitting assets in IRAs and Keoghs. Courts in community-property states (Arizona, California, Idaho, Louisiana, Nevada, New Mexico, Texas, Washington and Wisconsin) usually require divorcing spouses to share assets in those plans equally. Other states give judges more discretion, often to the detriment of lower-paid spouses. Judges in these states generally award as much as two-thirds of the marital property to the higher wage earner. Whatever your share, it probably won't be enough to finance the retirement you've been planning. Here's how a retirement stockpile dwindles in divorce.

**Defined contribution.** These plans may be 401(k)s, 403(b)s or SEPs (Simplified Employee Pensions) if you're salaried, or Keoghs and SEPs if you're self-employed. You may also have an IRA. If your plans and your spouse's are roughly equal in value, the court will likely let you both keep your plans intact. Otherwise, the judge may divide the total between you, instructing your employers in a court order which share belongs to each of you. Such plans are relatively easy to split up because they consist of company stock or money invested in securities. If the court divides your 401(k) in half, most companies will set up a separate account for your spouse's share. Henceforth, your contributions will go entirely into your account. Some companies will let ex-spouses withdraw everything in their accounts as lump sums that they can roll over into IRAs or take as cash. Other companies allow withdrawals over time, as with any retirement account. Either way, the law imposes no 10% penalty on withdrawals by ex-spouses who are younger than 59.5.

**Defined benefit.** To make things simple, many divorcing couples agree to let one spouse keep the traditional pension, while the other takes all or a portion of the 401(k)s and other defined-contribution accounts. If you must split a pension with your ex, most companies prefer you to use the so-called fixed date method. Here's how it generally works. Based on your salary and years of service, your benefits office will calculate what your pension would be if you were to retire on the day you expect your divorce to be final. Say you would qualify for a $10,000 pension on that date. A court might order your company to give your spouse $5,000 a year of your pension no matter how big your benefit actually turns out to be when you really retire. Your spouse would start to collect the $5,000 when he or she reaches retirement age (usually 65 though some companies permit earlier retirement) even if you're still working and not receiving your share of the pension.

Some companies let you use a more complicated calculation called the fractional method. Here's how it works. Divide the number of months you were married and employed at your company by the total number of months you've worked for your company, married or not. Next, multiply the result by your estimated pension benefit on the date you plan to retire. Finally, multiply that amount by the percentage of your pension the court has awarded to your spouse. Let's say you've been married 10 years, have worked at your company for 15 years and expect a $20,000 pension when you retire at age 65. Divide 120 by 180 and multiply the result (0.666) by $20,000, resulting in $13,320. If the court gives your spouse half your benefit, he or she would get $6,660 a year. You both take a gamble with this method, however, because you might opt to work beyond 65, thereby boosting your pension and your ex's share of it. If you take early retirement, your pension and your ex's share would be smaller. Whichever method you use, your ex can file for a cut of your pension at the earliest retirement age your company allows. But doing so freezes the amount your ex receives even if you continue to work and your benefits keep growing.

**Don't ignore Social Security.** An ex may collect up to 50% of the benefit a former spouse has earned when the ex begins receiving Social Security checks. When an ex files for benefits, Social Security automatically compares benefits from his or her own work record with benefits due as an ex-spouse and gives him or her the better deal. To get Social Security benefits as an ex-spouse, you must meet all four of these requirements: 1) your broken marriage must have lasted at least 10 years; 2) you must be 62 or older; 3) your ex must be at least 62 even if he or she isn't retired; 4) you must not be married to a new spouse.

 **Picking a Skilled Financial Planner**

As many as 72,000 advisers call themselves financial planners, and 90% claimed in a recent survey that they specialize in retirement planning. Sounds like a buyer's market? Not exactly. Many so-called planners don't know a rollover from a rollaway. But there are also some top-notch planners who can help you reach your goals if you don't feel you can design your own retirement plan. Try first to determine whether you need help from a planner, who is usually a generalist, rather than from a specialist such as an estate lawyer, a C.P.A. or an investment counselor. You need a generalist when you're trying to solve more than one problem involving, say, your company stock options, complex benefit plans and an ex-spouse residing in another state. To find a planner you can trust, you should start by taking these steps.

**Identify talented candidates.** Ask your accountant, banker or lawyer for recommendations. Or seek names from friends who have used planners and been satisfied with the results. Make sure the candidates have worked in the field for at least three years and use the title C.F.P. (certified financial planner) or Ch.F.C. (chartered financial consultant). To earn either designation, a planner has to take a number of courses in financial fundamentals and pass an exam.

**Interview them thoroughly.** During an initial meeting, which should be free, ask each planner about his or her experience and the types of services offered. Is the pro well-versed in areas that concern you, such as building a retirement fund or investing for income? Next, ask about payment. There are three types of planners. Fee-only charge about $2,000 to $5,000 for financial plans. Fee-and-commission receive flat fees of $600 or so for plans plus 3% to 5% commissions on investments that you buy from them. And commission-only derive all of their income from the 3% to 5% commissions on investments they sell to you. While salespeople may provide wise counsel, their chief interest is peddling products. Those who earn the bulk of their income selling products may have a conflict of interest that can bias their recommendations. Ask candidates to show you retirement plans for clients with goals and finances that are clearly similar to yours. You should make sure that you understand the plans and that they contain specific investment recommendations such as stocks and mutual funds.

**Do a background check.** To learn whether your top candidate has been subject to disciplinary actions, call

the SEC (202-942-7040) and your state securities department (it's usually part of the Department of Commerce,
which is listed in your phone book). If the adviser
belongs to the National Association of Securities Dealers,
ask the NASD (800-289-9999) whether there have been
judgments against him or her for such dubious practices
as requiring investment checks to be made out in his or
her name rather than to a bank, brokerage or fund company. Once you find a financial planner that you're comfortable enough to call your own, your work isn't over.
You still need to keep track of your investments and
always know what's going on in your accounts.

 ## Money's Outlook for Medicare

About $150 billion in savings is needed to shore up the
30-year old Medicare trust fund, the heart of the federal
health care program for the elderly. That amount would
rescue the hospital insurance trust fund, which is known
as Part A and funded by a 2.9% payroll tax. It would
also slow the rapid growth of Medicare Part B, which is
drawn from general tax revenues and beneficiary contributions to cover doctor visits and outpatient services.
Congress has a selection of savings championed by Rep.
Christopher Shays (R., Conn.). After reviewing that list,
we recommend the following steps toward strengthening
Medicare and saving roughly $130 billion.

**Make beneficiaries pay more.** Today's typical 65-
year-old retiree will get back $5.19 in health care bene-
fits over his lifetime for every dollar he paid into the
Medicare system. That's a pretty generous payoff and
one that could be reduced. Shays figures the government can save $95 billion by the year 2002 by doing the
following. First, raise the monthly charge that seniors
pay for Part B from $46 to $84, with higher-income folks
paying more. (The government would still pay for medical care for the poor). Second, increase the Part B
deductible, now $100 a year, to $150 next year and

# The Key Elements of Disability Coverage

Have you thought how your life would be upset if you were crippled in an accident? Even if you are nearing retirement, you shouldn't risk going without long-term disability insurance to replace lost income. Viewed as a surrogate paycheck, the policy's benefits should pay out an amount equal to 60% to 80% of your wages. Disability insurance is expensive. A no-frills policy covering 50% of the $75,000 income of a 40-year-old man might start at about $1,000 a year. The price could easily be twice that for a comprehensive plan that, among other things, replaces a higher percentage of income. Before shopping for a policy, check to see what disability coverage you have through your employer—it's usually 20% to 35% cheaper than comparable plans bought on your own. To keep your premium affordable and assure adequate coverage, you want a policy with these features.

◆ **A long waiting period.** Most policies don't start paying benefits until at least 30 days from the date the insurer says you became unable to work. Buying a policy with a 90-day waiting period can save you up to 20% in premiums. If you go out as long as a one-year waiting period, you could save another 11%.

◆ **Benefits paid to age 65.** It's not worth paying 25% more (if you're age 40, for example) to get full lifetime benefits. Instead, you should pay only for disability coverage until your retirement age, when Social Security and other savings can be your chief income sources. You also want a policy that can't be canceled and is protected against rate hikes. This is the only way you can be certain that the insurer won't drop your policy or make it unaffordable to you in the future.

◆ **A cost-of-living rider.** Raising your benefits with inflation will jack up premiums 20% to 25%. But you don't want inflation gutting your income when you're out of work. A 40-year-old would pay 14% more in premiums for an automatic 4% annual increase.

◆ **A residual benefit rider.** This lets you work part-time or in a lower-paying job. You then collect the income shortfall, which can total as much as the policy's maximum, from your insurer.

◆ **Own occupation coverage.** You could save about 10% on your premiums with an "any occupation" policy, which pays out only if the insurer determines that you're unable to work anywhere. Instead, you should shop for insurers that offer policies with "own occupation" coverage so that you'll get benefits if you can't do your own job anymore.

index it to the growth of Medicare spending. And consider requiring beneficiaries making 150% above the poverty line (about $10,660 for singles and $13,445 for couples) to pay 20% of the cost of lab and home health services, which are now free.

**Encourage seniors to join HMOs.** Only 9% of Medicare beneficiaries currently are enrolled in HMOs (health maintenance organizations) or other managed care plans, compared with 63% of Americans who have employer-sponsored health insurance. Some reformers would charge new beneficiaries an extra $20 a month, beginning around 1999, if they choose traditional care over a managed care plan. To achieve any real savings, however, Medicare must better manage its managed care arrangements. For instance, the government spends about 6% *more* on seniors who have enrolled in HMOs than it would have if they had stuck with a conventional plan. Medicare officials are working on adjusting the formula they use to pay HMOs. If it can then persuade at least half of all 37 million beneficiaries to join managed care plans, the government could save roughly $2.5 billion a year.

**Cut payments to providers.** Two ideas could save a total of $35 billion by 2002. First, reduce the generous reimbursement for certain outpatient services, such as ambulatory surgery and diagnostic tests. Second, slow the robust growth of spending on home health care, rehabilitation and skilled nursing care by giving hospitals a single payment covering both in-hospital and post-hospital care. This would eliminate the incentive hospitals now have to discharge patients quickly and send them into home health care settings where reimbursement is unlimited. Once the leadership in Congress endeavors to get Medicare back on its feet, the focus of reform should shift to restructuring the entire U.S. health care system. Otherwise doctors and hospitals, both already forced by Medicare to offer services to beneficiaries at discounts, will try to make up lost income by hiking fees for people who are covered by private insurance.

## Your Menu of Medicare Choices

You become eligible for Medicare at age 65, whether you're retired or employed. You automatically are enrolled if you're receiving Social Security benefits. Otherwise you must sign up at a Social Security office (listed in your phone book). You can enroll within a seven-month period that begins three months before the month in which you turn 65 and ends three months afterwards. If you miss the window, you will have another chance during the general enrollment period every January through March.

**Determining the costs you pay.** So-called Part A benefits cover care in hospitals, skilled nursing homes, your own home or a hospice for the terminally ill. Part B benefits pay for out-patient doctor visits and lab fees plus psychiatric and chiropractic services. Part A is free if you've paid FICA taxes for 10 years (not necessarily consecutive). Nonqualifying spouses are eligible once they turn 65. Otherwise you must pay for Part A at a recent rate of $183 a month if you've been employed at least 7.5 years or $261 a month if you've worked less than that. Part A picks up all basic hospital expenses, including medication, semiprivate room and meals, for up to 60 days after you've paid a deductible, lately $716. To get skilled nursing home coverage, you must be hospitalized for at least three days and enter a Medicare-approved facility within 30 days of leaving the hospital. Medicare pays all costs for 20 days.

Part B is optional. You can buy it for a recent $46 monthly premium, an annual $100 deductible and payment of 20% of all covered costs. If you're covered by an employer's or spouse's health plan, however, you should check first to see whether it's a better overall deal. Keep in mind that you can always enroll in Part B if your private coverage ends. Note that if you're not covered by an employer's plan, your premium will rise by 10% for each year that you delay signing up.

**Figuring how you must pay.** After you've paid your 20% share, doctors who participate in Medicare send your bills to the insurance company that serves as your carrier. (For a list of Medicare physicians near you, you should call your state's carrier. A local Social Security office can give you the number.) If you use a nonparticipating doctor, you'll have to pay all charges yourself, then wait a month to be reimbursed. Nonparticipating health care providers can't legally charge Medicare recipients more than 115% of Medicare-approved fees. If you decide to join an HMO, Medicare won't charge you Part B deductibles. In return, you usually get free check-ups, eyeglasses and dental care. Note, however, that such services aren't covered by Medicare. For more information on coverage, call 800-772-1213 to request a free copy of the Medicare handbook.

**Appealing a disputed claim.** If a doctor or hospital tells you that Medicare won't pay for the treatment you need, don't automatically reach for your checkbook. Appeal instead. Only about 2% of Medicare beneficiaries do so. Yet 80% of them win, says Diane Archer of the Medicare Beneficiaries Defense Fund, an advocacy group in New York City. She explains: "Many times doctors and hospitals aren't completely aware of the full range of Medicare coverage." In addition, a recent study by Congress' General Accounting Office indicates that whether you're reimbursed may depend on where you live. Here are two examples. Claims for chest X-rays were 900 times more likely to be denied if processed in Illinois than in neighboring Wisconsin. And payments for certain lab tests were thumbed down 1,400 times more often in Illinois than in California. The chief reason for the disparities seems to be that Medicare claims are handled by more than 30 private insurance companies. (They're called carriers when they deal with hospital claims and intermediaries when they handle out-patient claims.) These companies differ partly because doctors don't always agree about what's medically necessary. Some insurers also review claims more carefully than others and usually tilt in patients' favor. In making an appeal, follow these strategies.

♦ If you question a doctor's judgment that Medicare won't pay for treatment, ask for a written explanation and send it to your carrier for a second opinion.

♦ To challenge a hospital's payment decision, ask its billing office to submit an official claim to the carrier for determination. Or appeal to your local Peer Review Organization, a group of doctors who have contracted with Medicare to settle such disputes. Your hospital's billing office can tell you how to make the appeal.

♦ In disputes about Medicare services at a nursing home or agency involved in home care, you should send a letter explaining your appeal along with your doctor's evaluation of your condition to the Medicare intermediary. (The institution has the address.)

♦ Don't necessarily give up if your first appeal is denied. The official notice that you receive will explain how to carry your battle further. An administrative law judge settles disputes over charges between $100 and $1,000. District courts decide those topping $1,000.

**Saving on Medigap policies.** New regulations from the Health Care Financing Administration will reduce costs for many people covered by Medicare who must fill gaps in their health insurance. The regulations will correct a problem that Congress inadvertently created in 1990 when it prohibited insurers from selling Medigap policies, which can cost as much as $2,000 a year, to people who already had coverage, usually as part of retirement packages. The legislation, however, had an unexpected result. If your ex-company's policy was among those that only partly supplement Medicare, you couldn't buy coverage to fill in the holes. Instead, you had to drop your ex-employer's policy entirely before acquiring a new one. Thus, if you had free coverage that provided, say, a good drug plan but inadequate reimbursement of co-payments, giving up your employee policy in order to buy a more complete Medigap plan could cost an unnecessary $1,000 a year or more.

The new regulations will let insurance companies sell you the extra coverage after they've given you a proforma statement warning that such coverage may duplicate your existing insurance. (Insurers are still prohibited from selling you a second Medigap policy if you already have one.) To find out whether your ex-employer's policy provides all the coverage you need, call your benefits department. Policies that fall short often pay for prescription drugs, eyeglasses or dental care. But they don't pay the deductibles and 20% co-payments for hospital and doctor bills that Medicare doesn't cover. To fill the gaps, you can buy one of 10 standardized Medigap policies, identified by the letters A through J. These range from bare-bones insurance that pays only for those 20% co-payments to ones also covering skilled nursing care, at-home recovery, 50% of all prescription drug costs and preventive care.

Every insurer offers the same plans but at different prices. You can get descriptions of the plans from the Medicare-Medigap Counseling office of your state insurance department (the number is in your phone book). Once you determine your need, don't forget to shop around for the best price. And remember to compare how prices will rise as you age.

 ## The Top Deals in Health Insurance

Medical insurance remains the No. 1 problem for early retirees. Today, retired people in their late fifties must pay up to $5,000 a year for comprehensive health insurance until they reach age 65 and qualify for Medicare. This assumes both spouses don't smoke and are in good health. What's more, former employers are increasingly unwilling to pick up part of the tab. If your ex-employer doesn't offer adequate coverage, there are ways to make private coverage more affordable. If you need help, you can hire a professional service such as Wilkinson's Benefit Consultants (800-296-3030) to scour its database of nearly 1,000 carriers for the three plans that suit you best. Or call Quotesmith (800-556-9393) for 60 to 70 quotes from various carriers. That's a lot of choices. But the data are free because member insurance companies pay the fee. Here's our advice.

**Buy only coverage you need.** In general, a comprehensive policy should pay most doctor bills in full or in part plus the full cost of hospitalization and surgery (once you've met a deductible and any co-payment). The policy should also cover bills for catastrophic care (up to at least $500,000) and part of your costs for prescription drugs and home-based health care. To be sure your insurance will be there when you need it, you should buy a policy from a company rated A or A+ for financial soundness by A.M. Best (available in most libraries). You can reduce a premium by increasing your deductible, co-payment or stop loss (the sum at which the insurer begins to pay 100% of your costs). A typical individual plan with a $250 deductible costs around $515 a month. The same coverage with a $1,000 deductible costs about $390 a month. You can also save by cutting costly policy features you don't need, such as maternity coverage at $100 to $150 a month. Whichever policy you buy, make sure it's guaranteed renewable so it can't be canceled if your health takes a bad turn.

**Check out competitive group rates.** Group coverage is often cheaper than individual policies. Premiums vary with the type of plan, the number and age of the group's members and their general health. For instance, the 250,000-member National Organization for Women, which any man or woman can join for $35 a year, offers couples of any age comprehensive coverage from Banker's Life & Casualty for about $470 a month. If you own your own business or are self-employed, you also can buy group coverage. Unless you're pooled with thousands of people, however, you may not get an attractive rate. And group plans are required by many states to include a number of mandatory coverages such as pregnancy that older people may not want to pay for.

**Consider joining an HMO.** Group HMO plans cost at least 13% less than most traditional indemnity plans. In addition, there's a fee of $5 to $10 each time you visit the doctor and $2 to $5 for each prescription. Unlike traditional plans, HMOs cover routine physical exams and other preventive services. One drawback is that you can't choose your doctor unless your HMO offers a feature called point of service. This extra lets you see doctors who aren't members of your HMO, usually for a 30% co-payment. But it may also boost your premium by approximately 5%. Managed care alternatives that are commonly called preferred provider organizations (PPOs) let you choose from a list of participating physicians for roughly the same cost as HMOs with an option for point of service.

 ## How to Find the Best HMO for You

In the past five years, the number of Medicare beneficiaries who have signed up with HMOs has doubled. The allure is easy to appreciate. By joining an HMO, you receive all of Medicare's services without having to pay extra charges including deductibles that run as high as $800 a year, 20% co-payments for outpatient services or most costs for prescription drugs. In addition, HMOs offer vision, dental and preventive care that Medicare doesn't cover. The cost can be as much as $100 a month, on top of Medicare's standard $46 premium.

If you're tempted to sign up, you should first ask your present doctor whether he or she works with an HMO. By joining that one, you won't have to switch to a doctor on the HMO's approved list, a requirement of all HMOs. This so-called primary care physician (PCP) will oversee your medical care and authorize any services from specialists or hospitals. You'll have to pay higher costs if you want to see a doctor outside of the HMO's network or feel there's treatment you need and your PCP doesn't concur.

If your doctor doesn't work with an HMO, seek recommendations from friends who belong to one or call your state's insurance department for a list of Medicare HMOs in your area. The department can also tell you about complaints on file regarding an HMO. One potential problem is that most HMOs pay doctors according to the number of patients they care for, not according to the number of services they provide. Critics charge that this system encourages doctors to see lots of patients but give them little attention. Some HMOs also pay their PCPs additional income at the end of the year if they haven't referred patients to costly specialists. If you disagree with your doctor's decision regarding treatment or if an HMO refuses to pay for emergency care, you can consider filing an appeal. (The HMO will tell you how to do it.) Once you've identified a likely HMO, you should then call to interview a representative and get answers to the following questions.

✦ What medical benefits does the HMO offer besides those that are covered by Medicare? You should expect at least check-ups, eyeglasses, dental care and most types of prescription drugs.

✦ How long must you wait to see your physician? Don't settle for longer than a day or two if you're mildly sick and two weeks for a check-up.

✦ How much do I pay for someone unaffiliated with the HMO? A small number of HMOs charge members a deductible of $100 or so and a co-payment of at least 50%. Most others make you pay full price.

If what you learn about the HMO makes you comfortable, interview up to three of its physicians. Ask whether they can be reached easily by phone, day or night, and whether they like the HMO's hospitals and specialists. A sympatico physician should also ask you about your medical history and concerns. What happens if you join an HMO and subsequently become dissatisfied? You can drop out at any time, either by certified letter to the HMO or by completing Form 566 at a Social Security office. You'll still be protected by Medicare's regular coverage.

 ## Sign These Key Documents Now

Nobody likes to think about the possibility of one day becoming incapacitated. Yet the time to write down your wishes for medical treatment is while you're still in good health. Here are documents you will need.

A living will specifies your wishes for medical treatment if you become terminally ill and unable to communicate with your doctor. Trouble is, doctors can easily disregard a living will. Thus you should also sign a durable power of attorney for health care. It names a person as your proxy to make medical decisions on your behalf, including hiring or firing a doctor. Your proxy can act anytime you're unconscious, not just when you're terminally ill. The living will effectively acts as a guide for your proxy, giving him or her greater conviction when faced with a difficult decison. And you don't need a lawyer to draft either document. Give copies to your proxy, doctor and family.

A durable power of attorney, which should be drafted by a lawyer, names a person to oversee your financial affairs when you're incapacitated. Be sure to select your agents carefully because they can do a great deal of harm. For peace of mind, you should consider naming two agents and require signatures from both for all transactions. Or limit their reach to certain accounts. If you want your agent to deal with Social Security or the IRS, you must specify your wishes in the document.